KERRY—

Thanks for helping sustain
AKA's leadership role!.

Enjoy our new book!.

Gordon Holness

Albert Kahn Associates

Continuing the Legacy

Preface by
Gordon V.R. Holness
Introduction by
Grant Hildebrand

Editorial Director USA
Pierantonio Giacoppo

Chief Editor of Collection
Maurizio Vitta

Publishing Coordinator
Franca Rottola

Graphic Design
Paola Polastri

Editing
Aaron Maines

Colour-separation
Litofilms Italia, Bergamo

Printing
Poligrafiche Bolis, Bergamo

First published November 2000

ISBN 88-7838-071-7

Contents

Preface

by Gordon V.R. Holness, P.E.
Chairman and CEO

Over the past 40 years I have been fortunate to witness a multitude of changes to the architecture and engineering practices. New technology and increased access to information have impacted our profession dramatically. Client expectations are different. Overall, the professional has changed to become what few of us had envisioned.

As each major change has occurred through the decades, Albert Kahn Associates, Inc. (AKA) has chosen to take a leadership position -- to remain in the forefront. This monograph was created to tell the story of many of our achievements and demonstrates our evolution over more than a century.

Personally, my career in the industry began in my native country, England, when at age 16 I joined a local county council architectural department as a junior mechanical draftsman. In the late 1950s I moved to London where I completed my technical education at night and worked at a mechanical and electrical consulting firm by day. At that time, professional practice offices were generally small, proprietary and separate - a joint architectural and engineering practice was virtually unheard of. This London firm's practice involved mostly institutional and educational buildings, some new construction, and mostly, the renovation of London's incredible collage of historical buildings. It was here that I developed a sense of classical and traditional building design.

After my time in London, I spent five years in Canada - first in Toronto, and then in Windsor. While in Canada, I had the invaluable opportunity to participate in Toronto's growth explosion, and most notably on the main administration building for the Montreal Olympics.

This era introduced me into the yet embryonic field of environmental design and energy conservation, which became one of the driving forces in my career.

From Windsor, it was just a short ride across the Detroit River to my final career stop: Albert Kahn Associates in Detroit.

That ride took me to opportunities and challenges beyond my wildest expectations. In Albert Kahn Associates, I found a company with an incredibly rich history, coupled with openness to new ideas, innovation and creativity.

Albert Kahn Associates, Inc. (AKA) was founded in 1895 in Detroit, Michigan, by a self-taught architect, Albert Kahn. When he emigrated from Germany in 1880 at age 11, Kahn was uninstructed in English and destined never to enroll in an American school.

Kahn rose to become America's foremost industrial architect, a niche his peers shunned. His rise coincided with (and many say actually propelled) the growth of U.S. industry, particularly the automotive industry in Detroit. While he was known internationally as an industrial specialist, Kahn also excelled in designing non-industrial projects, including academic buildings, hospitals, office towers, plus mansions for Michigan's new industrial wealthy.

Though Albert Kahn's philosophy that "architecture was 90 percent business and 10 percent art" often brought criticism from peers, it did not detour him from creating highly refined designs that have withstood the test of time. Even critics like internationally recognized German architect Mies van der Rohe, who argued, "functionalism is the enemy of beauty," on occasion used functionalist, Albert Kahn designs as models for their own work.

Today, AKA continues in our founder's footsteps as a fully integrated, multi-disciplinary professional practice, with wide-ranging diversity, flexibility and responsiveness to customer needs. We continue to fulfill the aspirations of Albert Kahn and feel the era of the architect as the Master Builder, so eloquently practiced by Albert Kahn in the 1920s and 30s, is returning. From the time Mr. Kahn served so well in his role of master builder and pioneered industrial building design, the name Albert Kahn Associates has remained synonymous with leadership in the construction industry.

Traditionally, architects and engineers have thought of a "client" as the owner/occupier or end-user of their services. But as owners continue to seek input for strategic initiatives, business planning and single-source responsibility in facility development, AKA's services grow. Widely different teaming relationships and delivery methods are being used. With this, the definition of "client" in our industry has been turned upside down. Today, AKA's clients include everyone from financial executives and management consultants to construction managers, process consultants and even other architects.

Yes, our practice is changing. In the past, architecture was often about creating monuments, taming nature, controlling society and defining a permanent place in the profession. Today, architecture must move quickly with changing technology, embrace nature, envision facilities that have a finite or temporary life span, and be completely centered on the individual client's needs. Albert Kahn Associates has embraced this shift of emphasis in every business sector it serves.

For example, it is our belief that architecture must improve the human condition and advance society. This is clearly demonstrated by our industrial buildings, which literally "touch" millions of people daily. In addition to fulfilling functional and economic needs, our architectural creations serve people in their daily lives by nurturing their intellect, sense of style and desire for unity and order. In several areas around the world, the economic growth brought by the industrial facilities we are designing is literally changing the entire states where they reside.

Our work with Mercedes-Benz (DaimlerChrysler) and BMW in the United States has truly created new social worlds in rural environments in Alabama and South Carolina. Across the globe, the one-million-square-foot A-Class assembly plant we developed in Juiz de Fora in Brazil for Mercedes-Benz has resulted in an immense cultural change to the region. Like other cities directly affected by the automotive industry's global expansion, Juiz de Fora is actually being created around an industrial facility, almost overnight. It is, therefore, essential that changes such as these be managed with extreme sensitivity and care. A task AKA embraces.

In the health care industry, it is widely accepted that architecture can support and enhance the healing process. At AKA, we believe architecture should lift the human spirit, mind and body, as well as enhance daily existence. Within our buildings, we promote a fusion of the senses - visual, auditory, scent and physical. If our clients love the structures we design, it is because of the process we use, which is to embody the goals of the client into the design itself.

With accelerating health care costs continuing in the United States, many health care institutions are discovering the economics of outpatient care. At the forefront, AKA pioneered the development of freestanding ambulatory facilities in the late 1980s with the design of structures in suburban Detroit such as Henry Ford Hospital clinics and the Providence Medical Center - Providence Park. The latter appears in this monograph. Facilities like these provide virtually all of the services of a traditional hospital - minus the beds for overnight stays.

In the office workplace, we are witnessing significant changes, almost on a daily basis. To meet future needs, we have to ask questions such as, Who are our clients? and Who are they becoming? Hoteling, rather than permanent workspace, and furniture on wheels are becoming commonplace. More work is being done on laptop computers everywhere but in conventional offices. Vehicles for communicating with one another are expanding. Therefore, remaining flexible and creating architecture that can adjust and change is the driving force at AKA today.

Similarly, our education, commercial, and research and development facilities are all driven by a common influencing factor: the rapidly changing technology housed in these buildings. For instance, the Media Union at the University of Michigan, a high-tech "library of the future," provides not only books, but over 800 personal computers and more than 2,500 network connections for student users.

Also of extreme importance to AKA is our dedication to the redevelopment of returning urban centers such as Detroit. Our Urban Design and Planning Collaborative group was formed in response to Detroit's revitalization efforts and aims to set design precedence for the revitalization of urban areas across the U.S. In recent years, The Collaborative group has led several significant restoration projects, including the new home for the Michigan Opera Theatre - the Detroit Opera House. This building, designed in 1922 in the style of a European opera house, was left vacant for two decades, with 90 percent of the interior plaster shell and finishes destroyed by water infiltration and neglect.

As the project's interior, historical architect, The Collaborative group headed comprehensive rehabilitation and restoration to the hall and lobbies. We have depicted the details of the project in this monograph. As you will see, the transformation is truly mesmerizing.

Looking toward the future, AKA's Vision for the Future is predicated on the continued expansion of services to meet the diversified needs of our clients. Our technical resources and structure are ideal in this new era when owners have a growing desire for single-source responsibility. These entrepreneurial initiatives, both individual and collective, bring our teams new opportunities and challenges for leadership.

For Albert Kahn Associates, whether future directions are in the application of new design technologies, the use of the latest interactive graphic software, or penetrating new geographic or service areas, the potential for continued success will depend on our ability to take the lead. As leaders and innovators, we are ready to embrace technology, change paradigms and move forward. We will work as a team and partner with others for mutual success, as well as continue to adapt ourselves to meet the needs of customers, even if it means reinventing ourselves.

Yet with all these changes, stability and a foundation upon which to grow are key. That indeed is the greatest asset that AKA offers - a legacy of experience, integrity and commitment. I hope you enjoy the following pages.

The Factory of the Future

Introduction

It has been said that architecture progresses as a result of the interactions between two competing forces: stability and change. Throughout history, there have been reoccurring instances when societies have collectively challenged established paradigms and accepted modes of practice. Such clashes have been most prevalent at the fringe of transition, such as the dawning of a new century or the beginnings of revolutionary thought. In its midst, there existed an underlying tension due to the uncertainty of what was to come. Emerging, as a result, was the need to evaluate the past and scrutinize the ensuing future.

Architect Albert Kahn was one of the early inventors of the automobile factory in the early 1900s. Today, Albert Kahn Associates, Inc. (AKA) continues his legacy by leading the industry in factory architecture. We stay educated on the latest developments in manufacturing – aided by ongoing discussions with auto manufacturing futurists and visionaries who openly forecast significant changes in auto production.

Hence, we continue to develop a thesis on how such changes in production methods will influence the form of future factories. During this process, we have found the issues that receive the most attention are energy conservation, sustainability, recycling, customized/unique products and development of fuel cells.

Recognizing the dynamic relationships between buildings, manufactured products, and ownership, we feel designers will need to provide a variety of options to meet the needs of future manufacturing facilities. A condominium approach that includes participation by Tier One suppliers supports a "kit-of-parts" system to building design. Here, responsibility of the building becomes a cooperative effort of several corporate entities.

The condominium-type collaboration strategy is clearly gaining momentum in many emerging markets. This is exemplified by our project for Mercedes-Benz do Brasil, where sections of the building are actually leased to Tier One suppliers that provide the automaker with components and modules.

Within this chapter, the factory is the center of a discussion on modes of production, evolving processes, and the rate at which these occur. Inherent to each investigation are certain ideals thought to be fundamental to (automotive) factory architecture such as speed of construction, and the continuous need for versatility and flexibility. In the following sections we discuss the changing relationship between humans and the machines of the assembly line, new construction techniques, cost, performance, quality of the environment, life-cycle issues and the tools needed to explore the design possibilities for…

The "Factory of the Future"

Albert Kahn's Innovations in Factory Design.

The role that Albert Kahn played in shaping factory design in the United States has been given great attention. His impact was enormous. It has even been said that Kahn's career not only coincided with but actually helped propel the rise of modern industrial production.

Kahn's objective was to provide solutions to the evolving needs of his clients – provide innovative factory forms that accommodated evolving construction and manufacturing technologies.

Undoubtedly the most significant commission in Kahn's early career was his design of Henry Ford's first large plant – the famed Automotive Assembly Building, built in 1909 in Highland Park, Michigan. With his design, Kahn gave Ford exactly want he wanted: a massive factory that would consolidate all Model T production operations under one roof. The design featured an 860-foot-long, four-story factory of reinforced concrete that needed fewer interior supports than traditional construction. This opened up floor space that was ideal for continual changes in the placement of machinery.

It was at the Highland Park plant that Ford would soon perfect a new invention: the continuously moving assembly line. In this predecessor to the power-driven assembly line, Ford used gravity to assist in assembling the Model T. Raw materials entered by rail and were moved by cranes through a tall, central space to balconies at different subassembly stations. Partially assembled cars descended down from the beginning of the line on the top floor through an elaborate system of gravity chutes and conveyors.

Between 1912 and 1915 Ford perfected his vision of the continuously moving assembly line, and suddenly, the 12-hour job of building one chassis took only 1 hour, 33 minutes. In 1904, the world's entire automobile industry produced 22,000 cars; 10 years later, the Ford Highland Park plant alone produced almost 250,000.

Another major contribution by Kahn at the Highland Park plant was his transformation of the factory environment, which had previously been notorious for its dark, cramped and

almost prison-like atmosphere. Kahn illuminated the work area with roof monitors that brought in both natural light and ventilation, and a comfortable factory work environment was borne. Expansive sidewall glazing was also used as a result of the pioneering frame construction. With nearly a half-million square feet of glass in its walls and roof, the Highland Park plant was appropriately dubbed the "Crystal Palace" when it opened in 1910.

Kahn's innovative factories became the enabling factor in Henry Ford's drive to put America on wheels. And even more importantly, Kahn's resulting "American System" – the standardized building that best suited Ford's assembly lines – became a model for mass production around the world.

The Transition

Well after the conclusion of Kahn's remarkable career with his death in 1942, Albert Kahn Associates, Inc. (AKA) remains a worldwide leader in the design of factory buildings that respond to the manufacturing process. Our efforts concentrate on creating highly specialized, efficient, flexible and expandable factories that optimize process flow. Examples can be found in AKA's design of the Nissan Motor Manufacturing Corp. USA assembly plant in Smyrna, Tennessee and the BMW Manufacturing Corp. assembly plant in Spartanburg, South Carolina.

In creating the forms for future factory buildings, AKA carries on the tradition of addressing clients' needs by investigating the influences of the emerging requirements and changes in the manufacturing process.

Changes in Manufacturing Technologies

In today's evolving and highly competitive global markets, manufacturers are faced with the challenge of minimizing the cost of production while improving their manufacturing capabilities and product

quality. There are numerous responses to these challenges that range from innovative techniques for simplifying the manufacturing process to redefining the entire conceptualization of factories and what form they should take in the future. The design requirements of the factory of the future focus on how to incorporate a greater sensitivity to our environment and use of our natural resources for products. Emerging automated technologies in the manufacturing process is also key to future design. Terms like agile and "lean" manufacturing, environmentally responsible, integrated systems, computer-integrated manufacturing, concurrent engineering and robotic assembly are now commonly used when discussing requirements.

How will the aforementioned issues affect the factory of the future? For example, will factories continue to be designed in the traditional way – as a highly specialized building for a specific site and production line – or will there be new form-making strategies that respond to emerging manufacturing technologies?

We believe dramatic change is on the horizon. The factory of the future will have a set of requirements that are different from those of the past, and the development of new building types will be needed.

The task of rethinking the design of factory buildings involves reconciling not only the shift of present standards, but also the potential transformation of these ideals in successive years.

Given the demands of current technologies and practice, it can be argued that future factory buildings must have these important characteristics: to accommodate extremely rapid change, and to be able to grow and expand, or even downsize. Change and growth are not exactly new, however – in our industrial design experience, it has rarely been the case that a factory building will not be modified through its lifetime.

Human-Machine Interaction

Many are convinced that we are not far from fully automated, worker-less factory environments. Given the increasing level of automation in next-generation factories, workers with high levels of education may assume the role of supervisors, with highly specialized tools independently performing the routine and time-consuming tasks of assembly. The machine will always require maintenance by the trained mechanics, however the majority of the employees will be involved in the customization to meet the buyer's needs, which could entail

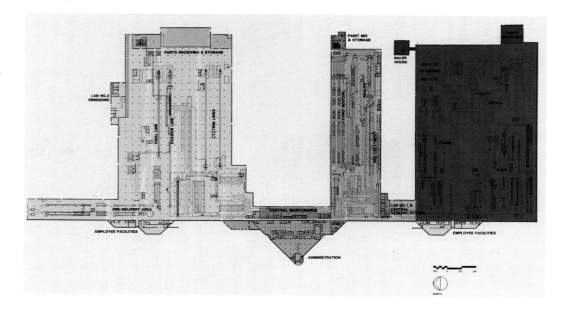

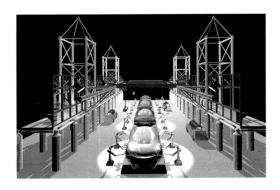

extensive support. As always, the relationship between people and machines in future factories will drive the arrangement of functions in the factory.

In contemporary factory buildings, the layout involves an integrated solution to the functional needs of the manufacturing process and the people who operate this process. The production line, and the structural, architectural, mechanical, and electrical systems are selected for appropriateness as to flexibility, expandability, cost, speed of construction, and availability in the local region of the project area.

The linear process of automotive assembly needs to be flexible and expandable. This is often accommodated by connecting production elements to a spine, while reserving space between the elements for expansion and access. This idealized solution leads to decisions concerning the amount of expansion that is to be provided for each component in relation to the constraints of the given site regarding size, cost and land utilization. It also provides the greatest available perimeter surface for logistics. Additional factors involve travel distances for personnel, management, and communication between elements and the related cost surcharges to solve these problems. This strategy is appropriate for the incremental expansion needs of emerging markets.

As an alternative to the aforementioned scheme in which parts are assembled along a spine, a more compact scheme, or a hub, can be achieved. This arrangement provides economical links between elements, opportunity to centralize production management and employee facilities, and more efficient land utilization. However, such arrangements are difficult to expand and grow.

In contrast to the above factory requirements, emerging manufacturing technologies introduce new possibilities for factory layouts and are likely to result in new factory types.

The relationship between workers and machines is also changing. Workers in future factories will not need to maintain direct contact with the production line.

This is in contrast to today's assembly line where supervisors commonly take active, close-up roles, as accommodated for in the design of the BMW assembly plant in Spartanburg, SC.

Here, painted vehicles pass right in front of the upper level production offices as they move to the assembly area.

Over the years, American industrial architecture evolved from the pioneering efforts of Albert Kahn in the early 1900s, where his single-story production floors with large sidewall glazed areas and glazed roof monitors created opportunity for natural lighting and ventilation.

However, in the 1950s and 1960s, the industrial factory evolved into the "closed box," featuring tempered air ventilation and artificial lighting. This scenario unfortunately denies the workforce contact with the exterior environment for most of the working day, resulting in de-humanizing working conditions.

The solution is to reintroduce day-lighting while creating new ways of introducing natural light into the workplace. For Mercedes-Benz' M-Class assembly plant in Alabama, AKA utilized saw tooth clere-story roof monitors that rise eight feet above the roof and allow natural light to enter, with minimal solar heat gain. Judicious use of natural lighting increases worker mental and physical wellbeing. Another benefit is that day-lighting provides points of orientation in what are typically very large buildings.

Construction: The Universal Building Concept

Generally, factory buildings are not

mass-produced but instead are usually uniquely designed for a particular program and a particular site. They are primarily based on product and process and have difficulty in accommodating new programs. This approach, unfortunately, is a gross waste of our valuable natural resources.

Tomorrow's factory architecture must be able to quickly adopt new manufacturing technologies such as widespread computerization, robotology, agile manufacturing, customization, global supply chains, and virtual work environments. New low cost, lightweight and prefabricated building types will be required. Factories will be assembled quickly and designed with the possibility of change in mind, a "Universal Building Concept".

The Universal Building Concept utilizes a "kit-of-parts" approach to design. The advantage of this approach is the development of a vocabulary of building elements that can be arranged in various ways to create different factory layouts adjustable to the requirements of specific sites. This approach allows for a far more ecologically sound solution considering the massive amounts of natural resources used in manufacturing. Facilities that consider reuse from the start might even be constructed by third party developers and leased out as condominiums.

A typical factory of the future needs to be dynamically re-configurable to support just-in-time manufacturing of custom and semi-custom products. Advances in robotics and remote control systems will allow these buildings to be quickly assembled and disassembled. Moreover, wireless networks will allow equipment and production equipment to be physically relocated without incurring the overhead of re-routing the connections between the parts. Wireless connections will reduce the cost of networked connections.

For our concept of the factory of the future, the plan is flexible and accommodates growth and expansion. As we illustrate in the chapter, a segment of the production line of a possible factory arrangement in which products are supplied from the sides and the delivered at the ends. The production line is fully automated and humans merely supervise the manufacturing process from the upper levels. The building elements are equipped with automation to permit quick rearrangement and change of building and manufacturing process components.

Conclusion

Although it is impossible to introduce a formula for designing future factories or even to predict how our factories will actually appear in the future, we have tried in this chapter to loosely sketch out ideas and possible approaches that may guide the decisions concerning future factory buildings.

We anticipate that the need for greater environmental sensitivity, coupled with emerging manufacturing technologies for products and building elements, will change the way in which factories operate and will very likely lead to new design solutions.

The challenge is to evolve the design process and allow it to accommodate the new demands.

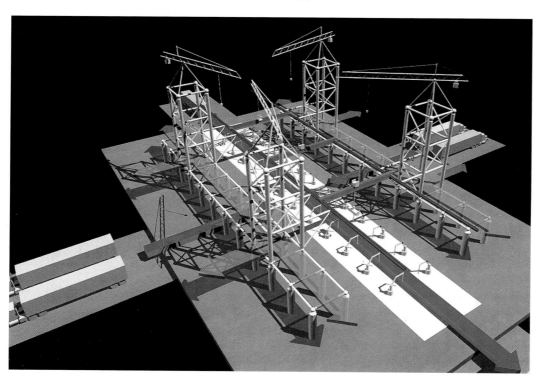

Albert Kahn and His Firm:
A Place in History

by Grant Hildebrand

At the beginning of the twentieth century, architecture for industry began to find its own character, to put forward its own dramatically contributive innovations. This coincided with a change in the Industrial Revolution itself, where rapid and less expensive production of familiar items – especially the motorcar – would affect every aspect of daily individual life.

This is international story of architecture in which American industrialists and architects played a vanguard role. Among those American architects, none had a greater influence on the development of industrial architecture than Albert Kahn – or, more accurately, the firm of which he was founder and director. Yet while, in the large perspective of historical significance, this was and continues to be the major contribution of the firm Kahn founded, it is not the only contribution. The firm's remarkably comprehensive body of work serving the needs of commerce, education, and health, can claim a significance in its own right.

Albert Kahn was born in 1869, in a small town near Mainz. He spent his childhood in Echternach, and came to the United States, to Detroit, with his family in 1880. His formal schooling ended with his immigration. In 1884, however, he was apprenticed to the excellent Detroit architectural firm of Mason and Rice, where he rose rapidly – by the age of 22 he held the position of chief designer. He worked in the then-popular mode of Richardsonian Romanesque, and did some work in the Shingle style, too; there is some indication that the famous front porch of the Grand Hotel on Mackinac Island is by his hand. From this experience he developed an admiration for Richardson and an even stronger admiration for McKim, Mead, and White. To those he would add, over the years, a familiarity with the work of Daniel Burnham, Eliel Saarinen, and Louis Sullivan, and would draw from each an inspiration for many projects of quality.

He founded his own firm in 1895. By 1903 he had secured a large project, the Engineering Building (now West Hall), for the University of Michigan. With this project he began an approach that would shape his emerging firm, and would be a key factor in its success. For he developed the project not as a sole "designer" but as leader of a team. A key member of the team was his brother Julius, a graduate of the University and developer of an early system of concrete reinforcement that was used for the project. In this Albert Kahn created a new kind of architectural practice for he was the first to bring architects and engineers together, working side by side, with shared authority, in one office with an integrated purpose.

For the same client in 1911 Kahn designed Hill Auditorium, following a trip to Italy where he sketched the brickwork of palaces and churches in Siena and Bologna. Hill was followed by a large number of structures for the University. The many projects of the 1920s included Angell Hall, a classic masterpiece and a major focal point for the campus; and the Italian Renaissance Clements Library, the building that, late in his life, Kahn would claim as his favorite among all his work. He also designed the General (now Graduate) Library, and the original University Hospital. In the late 1930s, Kahn designed the University's Burton Tower.

During these same years, his firm was establishing a reputation in commercial work as well. Among many such projects, the enormous General Motors Building in Detroit's New Center must be noted; completed in 1921, at 1.2 million square feet it was the largest of Kahn's commissions to that date. It was followed in the late twenties by the Fisher Building just across Grand Boulevard, and shortly thereafter by the New Center Building (now the Albert Kahn Building and the long-time home for the Kahn firm), a block north on Second Avenue.

Three of these projects demand further description. The distinguished critic Lewis Mumford has compared the locally famous acoustical quality of the University's Hill Auditorium to that of Adler and Sullivan's Chicago Auditorium, while Hill's exterior is a striking reinterpretation of Louis Sullivan's National Farmer's Bank in Owatonna, Minnesota, of 1908-09. The exterior organization of the General Motors Building is also indebted to Sullivan; it follows his early formula for the skyscraper, with its clear and elegant base, twelve-story intermediate office zone, and twostory crown. The plan, however – an

east-west spine with eight peninsulas of office space to north and south – derives from Daniel Burnham's humane realization that such an organization offers not only light and air to all offices, but pleasant outlook as well. The building is now a National Historic Landmark.

The Fisher Building is the third project that demands further description – demands, actually, a brief digression. In 1904, for Detroit newspaper magnate George G. Booth, Kahn designed a home Booth would call Cranbrook House, to be built on a large tract of rolling land well north of Detroit. In 1922 Kahn saw and was struck by the quality of the Finnish architect Eliel Saarinen's entry in the Chicago Tribune Tower competition of that year. Kahn supported an invitation to Saarinen to serve as professor of architecture at the University of Michigan. Booth, in the intervening years, had formed an ambition to build a school and art academy on the grounds of Cranbrook House; Kahn endorsed Saarinen as architect for the now-famous project. Kahn and Saarinen became friends, and Kahn's Fisher design is perhaps the finest of the many progeny of Saarinen's Tribune Tower scheme. (An interesting note is that the Fisher seems to have been inspired

more by Saarinen's later revised sketches than by the submitted competition drawings.)

To this record of educational and commercial work must be added a modest number of residences by Kahn's hand, though the residences themselves are in some cases quite un-modest. The most dramatically memorable of them is the Edsel and Eleanor Ford home in Grosse Pointe of 1928-29, for which Kahn traveled with the Fords to England's Cotswold Hills for inspiration and actual artifacts. On their return, on an extensive waterfront whose grounds would be landscaped by Jens Jensen, Kahn and the Fords created a home that is both grand and intimate, a mansion that paradoxically possesses a cottage-like ambience.

From early days, however, Albert Kahn exhibited another kind of architectural ability. In 1903 he was selected as architect for the Packard Motor Car Company. Three years later he did a remarkable automobile factory in Buffalo for the George N. Pierce Company, makers of the Pierce Arrow. Then in 1908 he was hired by Henry Ford to work out a new factory at Highland Park in Detroit to build the then-new Model T. Kahn seems to have found success in this kind of task because

of an ability to listen, a capacity for hard work, and an unusual talent for shaping and directing a team approach to problem-solving. And he possessed an intense enthusiasm for the new world of heavy industry.

The factory for Ford in Highland Park opened on New Year's Day of 1910. In its most visible exterior elevations it appeared to be a four-story building. At its core, however, was a single great space, four stories in height, within which sub-assemblies could be dropped one on top of the other, thus utilizing gravity to assist assembly.

The Ford Highland Park plant was, in the end, only a transitional type in the development of the modern factory, but it seems to have played a role in the origin of European Modernism. Reyner Banham has traced a chain of events behind Walter Gropius's widely accepted cornerstone of Modernism: the Faguswerk of 1911 at Alfeld. Fagus was a shoe-last factory; it was partly owned and supplied by the United Shoe Machine Company of

Beverley, Massachusetts, whose own reinforced concrete factory of 1903 was the work of Ernest Ransome. Banham claimed that in commissioning Gropius, Fagus put on his desk two photos: one of the Beverley factory, and one of Kahn's just-completed Ford Highland Park plant. There is some supportive evidence for Banham's claim; the clean frame of the Faguswerk might easily be argued as an offspring of the American work, the Ford plant especially; and Gropius would later refer to Fagus as "an American factory." But if the photo Gropius saw was the one shown here, he didn't see Highland Park's most important feature: the vast interior gravity-assembly chasm. And, more importantly, Ford and Kahn were about to take American industrial architecture in a much more promising direction.

At Highland Park, in March of 1913, Ford tried building the magneto by moving it, by means of a conveyor belt, past a series of fixed workers' stations, each with a specific and repetitive task. This was not the first assembly line, but it was the first in mechanized industrial production. The approach seemed promising. But it was obvious that such a manufacturing method was best served by a single working floor of extensive and indeterminate plan dimensions. This realization carried two other architectural implications. Prior factories had brought in light through wall windows. For a factory of broad plan dimensions that wouldn't work. But in 1906 Kahn and Lockwood, Green and Company had built for the George N. Pierce Company in Buffalo a factory of extensive horizontal dimensions for which light - unusually even light - was obtained through a glazed roof of saw-tooth configuration. Though the Pierce plant was built seven years before Ford's first assembly line, its broad roof-lit configuration was ideally suited to Ford's idea.

The one-story format also suggested a change in structural material. Concrete had been used for multi-story factories because of its fireproof nature and weight,

which helped to damper vibration. In a one-story factory, vibration was not as much of an issue since most equipment could rest on grade. Also, exit doors opened directly to the exterior, and risk of death from fire was radically reduced. Hence, the transition to a steel frame made sense. And it brought with it another advantage in its speed of construction, since there is no formwork to build, no meticulous placement of reinforcing, no curing time.

In 1917 Ford bought 2000 acres on the Rouge River, southwest of Detroit, to build a new industrial complex of potentially vast extent, intended for assembly-line processes throughout. Buildings were to be of one story and steel framed, and Kahn was to be primary architect. The Glass Plant at Rouge of 1922 is the epitomizing example of American industrial architecture at the time. The plan is crisp and simple, quickly laid out, economical of perimeter. The section is exquisitely tailored to the various light and ventilation needs of the annealing, grinding, and

polishing lines. The Glass Plant was the prototype not only for Rouge but – in a sense, and eventually – for the industrialized world. Its progeny at Rouge alone, all by the Kahn firm, included the Pressed Steel, Spring and Upset, and Open Hearth buildings; the Blast Furnances; the Rolling Mill; and the Coke Ovens.

How did this work at Rouge stand in relationship to other examples of industrial architecture?

In 1914 Fiat began design of a new factory at Turin that seems to have been completed in 1920. Constructed was a five-story version of Ford Highland Park of 1910. Its only real innovation was its banked-oval test track on the roof; manufacturing began at grade, with final assembly on the fifth floor. The Fiat plant was clearly intended to be a cutting edge design. Yet it failed to exploit the key feature of its model, the idea of gravity-assisted assembly – which, for Ford and Kahn, had itself become obsolete in 1913. We turn to England, birthplace of the

Industrial Revolution, and to the Royal Institute of British Architects Journal for February 1933. That issue focused on industrial architecture. All examples cited – 11 years after the Glass Plant at Rouge, 23 years after Ford Highland Park – were multi-story, concrete-framed factories.

The most dramatic testimony to the vanguard position of Kahn's industrial practice is found in the invitation to Kahn in 1929, from the Russian governmental bureaucracy, to establish a branch office in Moscow. This office was to design, and to train as well. In its three years of operation it produced construction documents for 531 factories and trained over 4000 Russian architects. Most of the factories were – originally – for production of farm tractors to serve Stalin's agrarian program. Most were also, by the firm's accounts, significantly overdesigned, perhaps in anticipation of a different production role at some later time of war.

Kahn's steel-framed factories of the 1930s demonstrate his unusual ability to create an architecture from uncompromised utilitarian demands. The Chrysler Half-Ton Truck Plant at Warren, Michigan, of 1937 (illus) is a famous example, crisp and elegant, spare and useful. Milton Brown, in American Art, chose a photo of this building as the frontispiece for his entire section on American Art between the wars, and said of it and its contemporaries, "Kahn's

various factories of the 1930s, notably those for General Motors and the Chrysler Corporation, exhibit a refined precision of architectural detail that is remarkable for the period…."

The Glenn Martin Plant at Baltimore, also of 1937, is of intrinsic interest for its vast column-free interior, 300 by 450 feet in plan, spanned by trusses of thirty foot depth. It also is of interest for its role in the later American phase of European modernism. Mies van der Rohe came to the United States in 1938. In 1939 George Nelson published The Industrial Architecture of Albert Kahn, and one of Mies's students at the Illinois Institute of Technology, Myron Goldsmith, recalls Mies poring over this book. Mies's work changed significantly at that time; he turned toward a greater interest in crisp revealed structure and above all steel structure. That the Kahn work had something to do with this is further supported by Mies's well-known proposal for a concert hall of 1942, a collage of wall planes over a photo of the grand Glenn Martin interior. Such contemporaneous appropriation of one architect's work by another is rare. It indicates in the appropriator a serious interest in the work appropriated. And it must be remembered that Mies was the utterly dominant influence in American Modernism of the 40s and 50s. Thus Kahn's late steel-framed factories contributed to the late and

pervasive phase of Modernism, as his early work may have contributed to its early European phase.

Actively at work until the last few weeks of his life, Albert Kahn died in December of 1942. By that date, of course, many firms other than his own had played major roles in the development of industrial architecture. Even so, Kahn, and more importantly the firm he had developed, can claim the key role in the story. At the time of his death the office had done hundreds of factories outside the United States and fully 2,000 in this country, accounting at times for 20 percent of this country's industrial work. The firm he had founded a half-century earlier had grown to include several hundred members. And the team structure of which he was a pioneer meant that that firm was organized around highly integrated teams of specialists in the many aspects of the architectural task; the ostensible head was really a leader among equals, as Kahn himself noted on several occasions. In part for this reason, Albert Kahn Associates continued without interruption a professional career built on the pattern of its founder.

The firm has continued its associations with its earliest commercial and educational clients. For the University of Michigan in the 1960s and '70s, Albert Kahn Associates was responsible for the Physics and Astronomy (now Dennison) Building, and a vast addition to the Graduate Library. For many years, the firm has been engaged in studies for adaptations and improvements to Hill Auditorium. In the early '80s, the firm designed the enormous, new Adult General Hospital, where it continues activity with numerous projects. Albert Kahn Associates designed the internationally recognized Media Union, a 250,000-square-foot high-tech library, and the East Ann Arbor Health Center, both constructed in the late 1990s. Several of these projects are described and illustrated herein.

Recent decades have spawned newer

educational clients, including Wayne State University, Michigan State University and Oakland University. Projects for many other health service clients have included additions and revisions for the Henry Ford Health System, Ascension Health, William Beaumont Hospitals and Johns Hopkins Hospital, to name a few.

The firm is also in a remarkable situation as it finds itself in the position to revisit the masterpieces of its founder. In the 1970s Albert Kahn Associates transformed the stables at the Edsel and Eleanor Ford estate into a visitors' center, as the estate passed into public stewardship. The firm's continuing involvement with Hill Auditorium has been noted. And in 2000 and 2001, the firm is executing a total adaptation of the General Motors Building for occupation by an estimated 4,000 employees of the State of Michigan.

Most appropriately, the firm continues a vanguard role in industrial architecture. Some of Albert Kahn's early clients still call on the firm's services, as in the case of the DaimlerChrysler Indiana Transmission Plant or the Ford Research and Engineering Center, described herein. But new technologies have changed the criteria for industrial architecture and so have changed its characteristics; new projects for old clients do not look like old projects for old clients. And new economics have changed the names of the players. Were he to return to his desk today, Albert Kahn might recognize the names of some of the more recent industrial clients of Albert Kahn Associates: BMW and venerable Mercedes Benz, for example – though DaimlerChrysler might be a surprise to him. Other clients – Volkswagen, Nissan, and Toyota – corporate entities of a later age – would be entirely unknown to him. But he would immediately recognize in the current firm some continuities too: a breadth of professional expertise and responsibility; and a commitment to the essential value of teamwork. Perhaps above all he would appreciate the continuing sense of excitement to be found in the firm's responses to the fast-paced and changing marketplace of the new century.

Works

University of Michigan University Hospital

Completion date
February 1986

Owner
The University of Michigan

Architect/Engineer
Albert Kahn Associates, Inc.

Construction Manager
Barton Malow/CRSS

Landscape/Master Site Plan
Johnson, Johnson, & Roy, Inc.

Material Handling Systems
Shotwell-Anderson

Elevators & Pneumatic Tube Systems
Lerch-Bates

Equipment Planning
PMS/RHA

Dietary/Food Service
Romano-Gatland

Programming
Coopers & Lybrand

Photographers
Beth Singer, Balthazar Korab

The University of Michigan's University Hospital, seated atop a bluff overlooking the Huron River and the city of Ann Arbor, is considered a crown jewel of its kind, thanks to its maximum efficiency, energy savings and the technologies it employs. It is the clinical care centerpiece of the University of Michigan Health System, which consistently ranks among the best health care institutions in the United States. The hospital, which also plays a large role in the research and teaching missions of UMHS, was completed in 1986 with a capital budget of $210 million.

Winner of the ASHRAE National Energy prize in 1989, the University Hospital was planned in 1980 and completed in 1986.

The 102,000 square meter (1.1 million square foot), 586-bed hospital is divided into two different composite parts. The inpatient beds are concentrated in a single, six-level tower, with each floor featuring intensive, intermediate and acute care nursing units in a linear arrangement. The hospitals' 61,300-square-meter (660,000-square-foot) base houses diagnostic and treatment, support and service facilities. This formal solution of long-span construction allows for a flexible space adaptable to ever-changing medical technology. The various care units are aligned identically on each floor and are supported on all six floors by a central nurse's station which manages intensive care with a thirty-two bed capacity.

The hospital supplies both basic medical services as well as high-level surgical operations thanks to its twenty fully-furnished operating rooms which provide for cardiological surgery, neurosurgery and organ transplants. The horizontal body is low and long and runs around the tower for 61,300 square meters. This space contains the treatment center and diagnostic laboratories; it's formal solution has allowed for a flexible space adaptable to new medical technologies and sophisticated instruments. This project also includes a modern two hundred and fifty seat auditorium designed for educating medical personnel.

The mechanical and electrical distribution is positioned inside the interstitial spaces positioned above each floor allowing any system modifications to be carried out without interrupting the adjacent working areas.

Energy use in the entire system is centralized: verified and controlled from a single operative area in order to obtain maximum energy savings. One important element in the management program is the energy conservation which takes place in an underground thermic basin. Filled with 7.6 million litres (two million gallons) of water, the basin serves as a liquid resevoir for cooling or heating the thermic energy used in the hospital. The hospital administration has registered an average occupancy of three thousand two hundred people per day including both patients and staff and an average daily transitory flow of ten thousand people including staff, students and visitors. The edifice as a whole easily manages this enormous human flux thanks to a distinctive division of the volumes allowing two flow types: professional and general public.

The hospital is constructed with brick and prefabricated concrete panels mounted on a steel structure which provides for ample glass window areas.

The critical southern exposure facades are isolated using a grey veneer and reflective windows.

The building is completely isolated in order to reduce heating increases and the overall heat loss falls below 50%-the maximum established by the Michigan energy code.

Patients and visitors travel through barrel-vaulted glass passageway, which connects the various medical annex buildings to the main hospital complex.

Left, the large cafeteria is divided into smaller sections for acoustic and visual privacy.

Below, the main circulation spine. The linear metal curved ceiling redirects light from continuously uplighted coffer.

Right, the main visitor lobby rises two stories under the undulated balcony, pictured below, which leads to the teaching auditorium.

The 586-bed University Hospital spans over one million square feet.

Brick expresses the four lower-level diagnostic base. Above rises the contrasting, six-story inpatient tower.

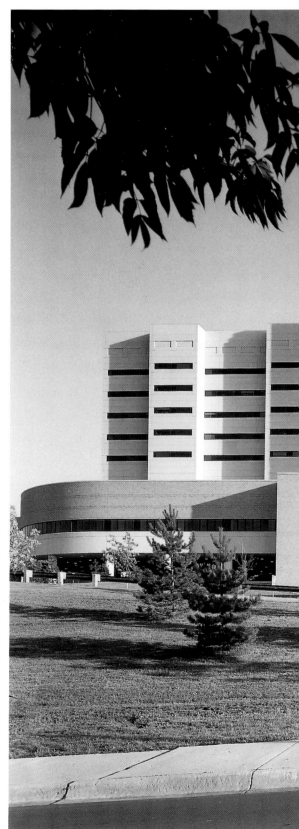

Providence Medical Center Providence Park

Phase 1A & B

Architect/Engineer
Albert Kahn Associates, Inc.

Construction Manager
George W. Auch Company

Landscape Consultant
Grissim/Metz Associates

Completion date
1992

Phase 1D

Architect/Engineer
Albert Kahn Associates, Inc.

Construction Manager
George W. Auch Company

Photographer
Lazslo Regos

The entire Providence Hospital complex extends over an area of 93 hectares (230 acres) that includes a golf course, six vast ponds and ample woody grounds. These elements provided the environmental amenities upon which the project was structured.

The first projectual part was finished in 1992 and includes the 8,360 square meter (90,000 square foot) MOB Medical Office Building and the two-story, 4,200 square meter (45,000 square foot) edifice containing space for diagnosis and the treatment center.

The MOB houses thirty-two patient examination rooms each of which is outfitted with modern technologies and sophisticated instruments. Other hospital services including a 24-hour emergency room, various medical sections and spaces for specialized cures are located in the other part of the building. The entrance, used by both medical structures, is resolved with a two-story atrium illuminated by an enormous skylight. Warm, colored bricks are united with leather-yellow Indiana calcareous rock for the facade. The choice of materials combined with the long ribbon windows and the simple, natural pathways creates a warm and comforting atmosphere for guests of the treatment center.

The extremely modern Michael and Rose Assarian Cancer Center represents one of the most technologically-advanced medical centers specializing in cancer treatment. Established with the help of Doctor Bill McLaughlin, director of the center, it contains the most advanced treatment systems, the most sophisticated diagnostic machinery and above all a physical, psychological and spiritual assistance program made available to patients and their families.

Inaugurated in August of 1999 at a cost of $16 million, the building has a total volume of 3,100 square meters (33,500 square feet) and can host two thousand patients per year. The new institution outlines the intentions of Stephen Whitney, director of architectural services for Albert Kahn Associates: "We tried to translate the idea of the patient's voyage into cancer, describing the physical and psychological passage which the patient travels in the course of his illness."

The space is intended to heal the spirit as well as the malady, offering multiple areas where patients can deal with their illness on every level: spaces for reflection, places for prayer, art rooms, zones for group therapy and for studying the individual pathologies.

The access area is resolved through a powerful geometric figure: an entirely glass-encased conical trunk standing 12 meters (40 feet) high with a 12 meter diameter at the base. Several stone sculptures are on display here and it is possible to admire the vast garden and lake which surround the center. The chemotherapy rooms look out on the same panorama, the green thereby becoming a background for the sculptures-works of art which can symbolize pain and sadness but most of all represent the patients' personal recovery.

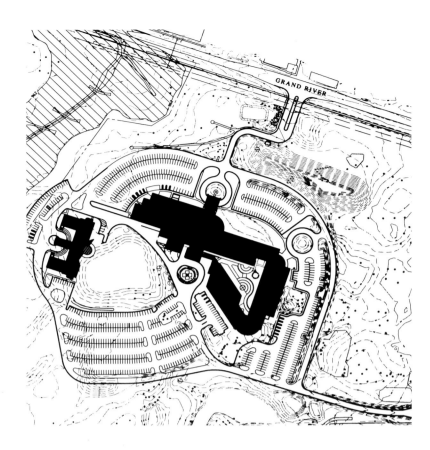

Left, site plan.
The 230-acre site
includes woodlands,
seven ponds and
an 18-hole golf course.

Right, Assarian Center
floor plan. Below,
the landscaping and
soft forms of the initial
building phase.

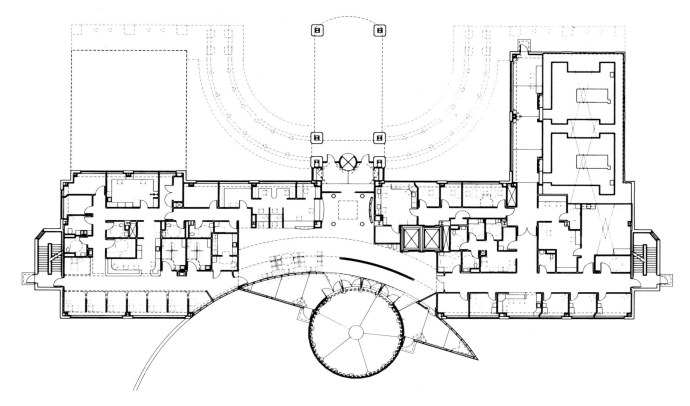

Left, registration cubicles. Below and right, the Assarian Center's resource library and dramatic reflection space. The roof of the two-level cylinder slopes from 44 to 15 feet and features a sloping skylight system.

Below, main entrance to the ambulatory care facility. Right, the porte-coshere canopy provides a sunny, friendly entrance element.

Ethyl Corporation Research Center

Completion date
August 1994

Architect/Engineer
Albert Kahn Associates, Inc.

Construction Manager
Turner Construction Co.

Mechanical Contractor
Colonial/Hungerford

Landscape Design
Grissim/Metz Associates

Photographer
Timothy Hursley

The Ethyl Corporation complex extends for 23,200 square meters (250,000 square feet) on a six hectare (16 acre) area. Constructed to consolidate research with administrative headquarters, the building provides the environment for research by one of the world's top suppliers of fuel and lubricants additives.

One of the purchaser's fundamental requirements was historical respect for the site, which was originally home to a penitentiary designed by Benjamin Henry Latrobe in 1797; another was to have maximum functionality united with modernity in the spaces where experiments are carried out on new products.

The entire $70 million project is composed of four highly technological volumes each outfitted based upon their productive functions: An edifice destined for offices and laboratories, a building with mechanical laboratories, a third for fuel mixtures and the last for industrial treatment of waste products.

The building projected to house offices and laboratories was completed with a six-floor tower connected to the volume by a horizontal development which contains the mechanical laboratories. Here sophisticated tests on petroleum products are carried out and transmission fluids, hydraulic fluids, lubricants and fuels are developed. These activities are supported by a ventilation system for the entire volume capable of removing all emissions produced by the running motors.

The formal solution that connects the office/lab building with the mechanical laboratory building is a long corridor, illuminated by skylights; a kind of internal road that manages the flow of employees as they move from one pavilion to another. This allows everyone from specialized engineers to qualified workers to interact with one another. The ducts, tubing and conduits are also housed inside this long space in order to facilitate eventual maintenance.

The welcoming area is resolved with a vast hall capped with a large copper dome that has a base measuring 12 meters (40 feet) in diameter and a height of 4.5 meters (10 feet).

The materials utilized include prefabricated concrete in the load-bearing parts, granite aggregate, limestone and copper present both in the lobby "curtainwall" and dome. The grey glass is united at the edges with mounted joints and works with the white panels, placed at the same level as the metallic parts, and the skylights of smoked glass to isolate the atmospheric agents and create internal spaces of a high technological level. The architecture created through the combination of these materials embodies the original project and expresses daily the labor of innovation and development undertaken inside the edifice, presenting an example of modernity and promoting union between architecture and industrial research.

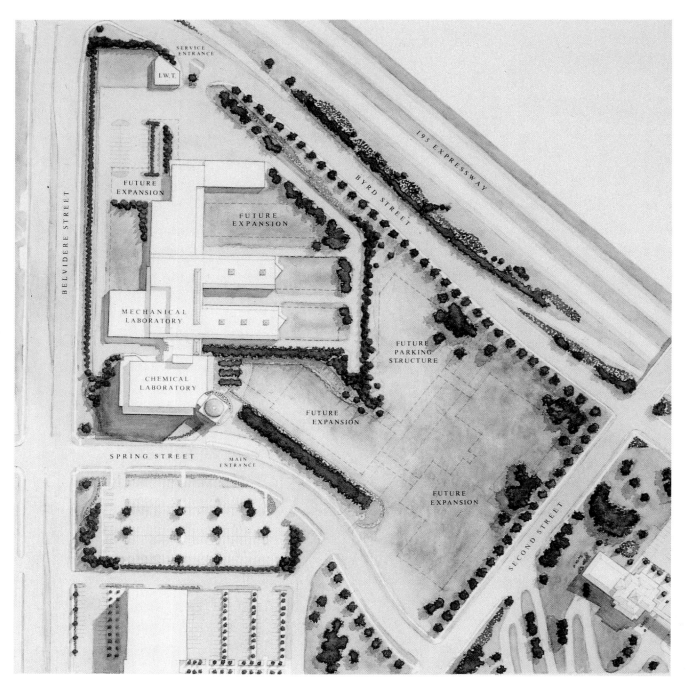

Below and right,
the reception center.
The coffered interior
of the dome is clad with
fabric-covered acoustic
panels. The polished
brass handrails of the
ornamental, winding
stair glide gracefully
up along curved glass
panels.

The main entrance leads to a three-story-high, copper domed reception center. Exterior illumination of the glass curtainwall facade creates a striking landmark on the Richmond skyline.

BMW Corporation Manufacturing Plant and Visitors' Center

Completion date
July 1994

Owner
BMW Manufacturing Corp.

Lead architect/engineer
Albert Kahn Associates, Inc.

Associate architect/engineer
Simons Engineering

Structural Engineer
Albert Kahn Associates, Inc.

Mechanical Engineer
Albert Kahn Associates, Inc.

Electrical Engineer:
Albert Kahn Associates, Inc.

General Contractor
Fluor Daniel

Construction manager
Hanscomb Harbert

Landscape Architect
Innocenti Webel

Delivery method
design/bid/build

Photographers
Balthazar Korab, Christopher Lark

For its first automotive manufacturing plant in the United States, BMW selected Albert Kahn Associates to create an environment that would foster the production of a high quality product. The concept of visual and verbal communication, used to foster the production of a high quality product, was the basis for the plant's configuration: a single, "under-one-roof" solution.

The project extends for 121,000 square meters (1.3 million square feet) on a property of 420 hectares (1,039 acres). The design parameters were developed interactively between the design team and key representatives from the owner's management, engineering, and process development in Munich, Germany. Further information was developed in Spartanburg with the design team, the owner, and local and state officials.

The three major manufacturing components – assembly, body and paint shops – are incorporated in an "L" configuration, a design to maximize adjacencies for the three shops as well as for the production offices, which are located at the L's elbow. This central area consolidates offices for all the three shops. Glazed walls give the office workers direct views onto the shop floors. This building layout replaces the commonly used "E-plan" or spine-like configuration for automotive plant design where the body, paint and assembly functions are interconnected-but-independent buildings.

In the foreground of the plant and serving as the principal interface between the owner and the general public is the futuristic Zentrum. A cresent-shaped, 2,800-square-meter (30,000-square-foot) visitor's center and museum, the Zentrum was designed to project a strong, positive and timeless image of the company to the public.

The true geometry of the Zentrum is formed by a radial inner wall and a spiral formed outer wall. The roof is 12 meters high (40 feet) at its apex, and slopes to five meters high (18 feet) at its leading edges. It is supported by exposed radiating trusses that span the inner and outer walls, providing a column-free display area for BMW products – both historical and future concepts. The displays occur processionally around the length of the plan, with the display complemented by the landscaped courtyard visible through the fully glazed inner wall separating them. The interior of the roof structure was left exposed to recall the industrial nature of the plant, and provides support for hanging displays and lighting.

The multi-use Zentrum also houses a 250-seat auditorium, meeting rooms, a gift shop and a snack bar. The building is clad in aluminum panels with a white, high-gloss, powder-coat finish.

The project was the recipient of an AIA Michigan Honor Award, where the jury expressed special recognition for the Zentrum as a place where "day and night, water and light are in harmony."

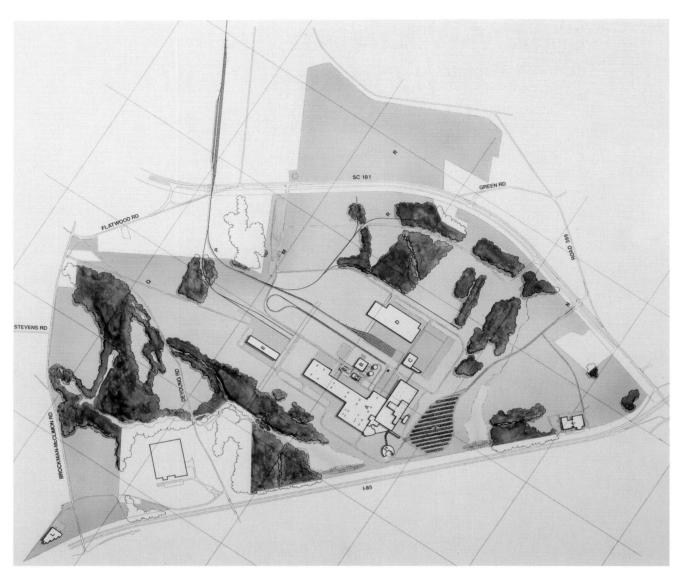

Left, site plan. Below, the opening in the Zentrum's cresent reveals to motorists a full-height glazed wall that faces a landscaped courtyard with fountains. Right, a covered walkway connects to the plant.

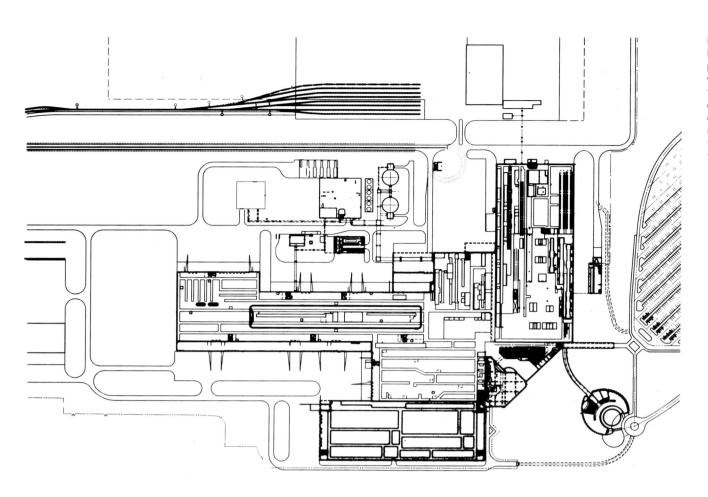

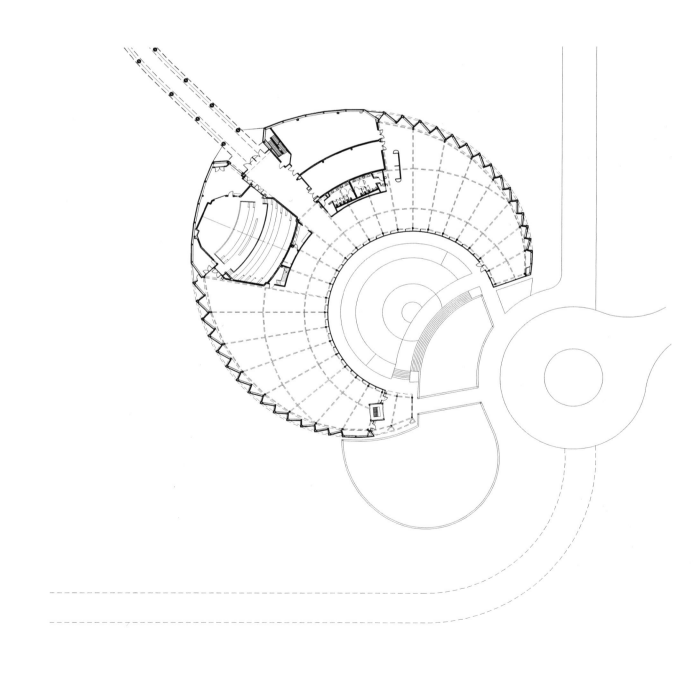

Left, the Zentrum's perimeter wall is formed by radiated piers, which create ever-changing views and light patterns. Below and opposite, the plant's communication plaza, where vehicles are transported by an overhead conveyor system.

Aurora Health Centers

Prototype ambulatory care center/medical office buildings

Completion dates
July 1994
(Aurora Medical Center, Kenosha, WI)
Sept. 1995
(Aurora Health Center, Waukesha, WI)
Owner
Aurora Health Care, Inc.
Architect/Engineer
Albert Kahn Associates, Inc.
Construction Manager
M.A. Mortenson Co.
Developer
Hammes Company
Photographer
Eric Oxendorf

Aurora Health Care Inc.'s goal with creating the Aurora Health Centers was to increase patient visits by providing lower-cost care to growing communities in Wisconsin. Serving as Aurora's program manager, the Hammes Company conducted a national search and selected Albert Kahn Associates, primarily because of its success in designing Providence Medical Center's ambulatory diagnostic and treatment center in Novi, Michigan, in the early '90s.

The Aurora Health Centers feature "one-stop care" with a focus on primary physician services. The challenge of the project was to create a prototype facility design that could be modified to fit sites of varying size and shape, and constructed in a modular basis. This design was first introduced with the Kenosha facility by placing its two major components – a three-story, 8,360 square meter (90,000 square foot) medical office building, and a single-story, 5,100 square meter (55,000 square foot) ambulatory care center – on opposite sides of a lobby "hinge." For future ambulatory care centers, such as that which occurred in Waukesha, the two areas could be constructed in different orientations to the lobby, thus allowing the basic design to be modified to fit infinitely different size parcels of land.

The ambulatory diagostic and treatment center provides extensive medical tests and procedures for those patients who require such care. The wing also includes an ambulatory surgery center that can treat over 4,000 patients per year. Here, patients who need more extensive medical tests or procedures can receive treatment and go home the same day.

The medical office building features physician suites finished to suit doctors in private practice. The design enables physicians to expand their suites into adjacent space with minimal renovation work.

The designer's goal for the design of the Aurora Health Centers was to create "healing" architecture. The concept is a comfortable, timeless architecture that projects a permanent image of long-lasting grace and simplicity. Designers used colorful interior finishes, comfortable seating and carpeting, and ample natural light in public areas to create a warm and supportive environment. To facilitate wayfinding, the central lobby and major corridors are located along exterior windows, and diagnostic services can be accessed directly from the lobby.

The main canopy of the Aurora Health Center rises over a two-lane entrance road. The circular barrel vault canopy, constructed of translucent fiberglass panels, allows daytime light and sunlight to softly filter through the panels. In the evening, lights around the inner canopy perimeter uplight the barrel vault making the panels glow in the dark. Concrete bollards accent the entrance curb lane.

The building's exterior materials feature red brick and cast stone trim, complemented by modern-looking, green-tinted glass. Illuminated skylights over the lobby mark the entrance at night.

Below, the Aurora Health Center's main canopy rises over a two-lane entrance road.

Right, the red hard burned brick contrasts warmly with the precast concrete panels and window trim. Recesses in the brick and concrete sections add visual interest to the facade.

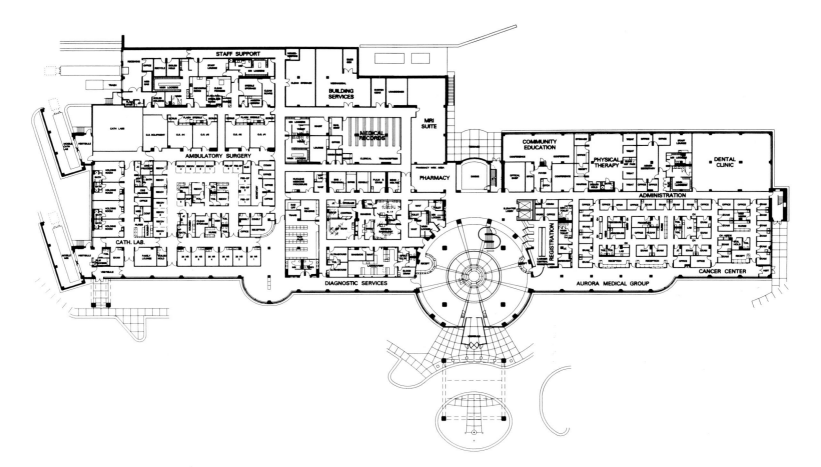

Above, first floor plan.
Below, the medical
office building offers
expandable suites for
private and clinical
physicians.

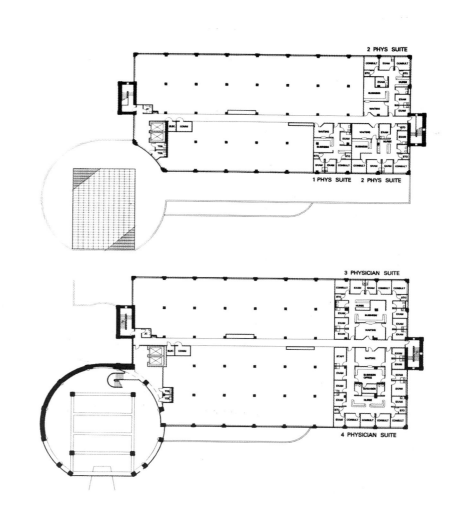

Above, a large circular reception center acts as a hinge to connect the two major components of the facility.
Left, clinic entrance.

The Aurora Health
Center at dusk.
The building facade
is softly uplighted
to enhance the warm
red brick walls and
contrasting concrete
piers trim.

University of Michigan Media Union

Completion Date
June 1996

Owner
University of Michigan

Architect/Engineer
Albert Kahn Associates, Inc.

Interior Designer
Albert Kahn Associates, Inc.

Landscape consultant
Johnson, Johnson, & Roy

Acoustical
Acentech

General Contractor:
Ellis-Don Michigan Inc.

Photographers
Gary Quesada @ Hedrich-Blessing

Built to change educational formalities, this library is the result of advanced technologies developed with the resources of four university departments: Architecture and Urban studies, Art, Engineering and Music. Located on the University's north campus, this new volume is structured around modern technological spaces within which information laboratories can be created and a new concept of a culture can be developed based on the utilization of media.

The building volume is organized on four floors for a total volume of 23,225 square meters (250,000 square feet). The 750 computer stations are distributed on different levels and can host as many as 1569 students. There is an enormous library with a 500,000 book capacity.

The first floor houses the interdisciplinary activities with direct access to production spaces: audio and visual resources for creating artistic material, virtual reality and 3D laboratories, classrooms for teleconferencing and an exposition gallery.

The library is located on the ground floor, and is filled with mechanical and electrical equipment as well as, naturally, books. The second and third floors host workstations for computer research, private classrooms for students, group-study areas and spaces for learning how to use the computer.

The building is developed on a square plan articulated by a series of 15-meter-high (50 feet) columns with, on each floor, a large window facing the campus.

The interior contains the same columns, outfitted with identical materials: red brick and Mankato stone.

The light studio is a fundamental element of the project: all the spaces intended for work on the personal computer are illuminated with artificial light and the points of light are positioned in a uniform manner in order to allow the emplacements to be shifted and moved around freely. The corridors and communal spaces are awash with natural light that arrives through long windows or from any of the twenty-two pyramidical skylights positioned above each column. Through these zenithal openings seventeen internal spaces were created, brightened with natural light and positioned most of all in the distribution and exchange flow zones.

The grand hall on the last floor receives light from the 335 square meter (60 foot square) glass-covered roof.

The library takes advantage of its position on the campus. It is physically located between two other university buildings and thereby functions as a "bridge"–a formative connection between different university disciplines–wherein students can collaborate, conduct research, experiment and create new expressive products together. A new simplicity characterizes this construction: studying, teaching and experimenting become activities readily available to every student. Just as with exchanges and the development of the creative process the role of the book is mutating to adapt itself to modern times.

Below, site plan.
The 250,000-square-
foot library is the focal
point of the University
of Michigan north
campus.

Upper right, section.
Lower right, each entry
is characterized by the
arrangement of an
unbraced, 50-foot-tall
brick columns with
limestone caps.

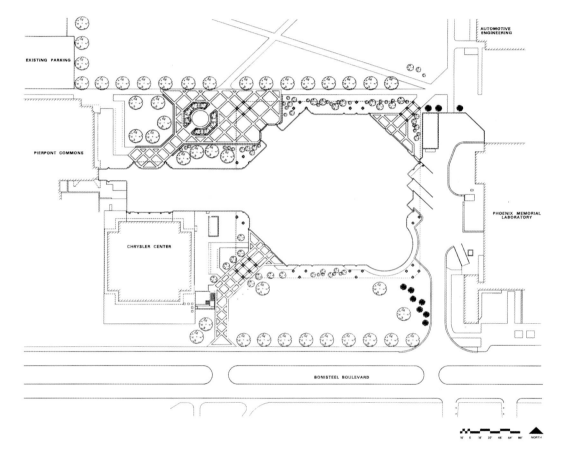

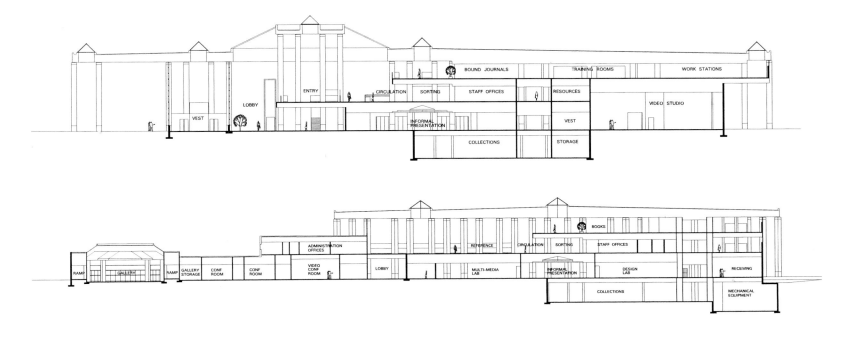

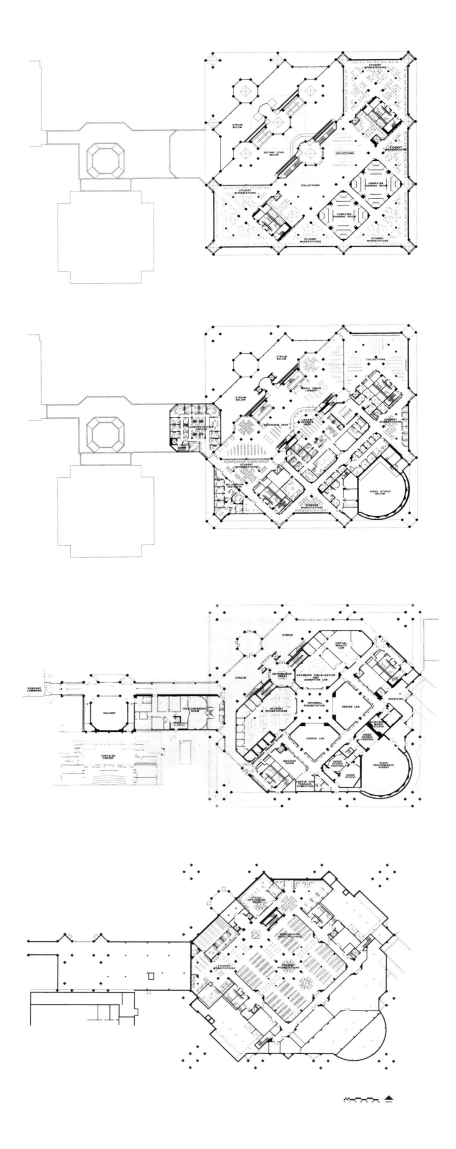

From top: plans for the third, second, first and basement levels.

The space plan locates audio, video and performance spaces on the first floor, clustered around a lounge. Computerized workstations and traditional library components are located on the upper and below-grade levels.

The video
teleconferencing room
provides an unlimited
arrangement of seating
and viewing
opportunities.

The play of natural lighting against the indirect lighting accentuates the brick columns. Opposite, the stark white mass of the atrium elevators is contrasted against the brick and stone columns.

The gallery shows work from the University's school of Art and Design. The versatile space can also be used for events such as science fairs and conference receptions.

The vertical brick columns stretch upward to support the 60-foot-square skylight that provides natural light into the atrium.

Mercedes Benz M-Class Assembly Plant

Completion date
August 1996

Owner
Mercedes-Benz U.S. International

Architect/Engineer of Record
Albert Kahn Associates, Inc.

Associate Architect
Gresham, Smith and Partners

Interior Designer
Albert Kahn Associates, Inc.

Engineers
Albert Kahn Associates, Inc.

Landscape Architect
Grover & Harrison

Lighting
Albert Kahn Associates, Inc.

Acoustical
Albert Kahn Associates, Inc.

Kitchen Consultant
E.F. Whitney

General Contractor
Fluor Daniel

Photographers
Gary Quesada @ Hedrich Blessing,
Glen Calvin Moon

The new Mercedes Benz factory intended for the construction of its "M-Class" cars is located on the land of three old farms occupying a total of 386 hectares (966 acres).

In order to produce 70,000 cars per year a refined and efficient industrial system was created, concentrating the planning on several basic concepts. For the entire 92,900 square meters (one million square feet) of the project the central objectives are constructive quality, communication and interaction.

The three principle volumes of the rectangular plan-the area for structural formation, the area for painting and the area for final assembly-are united under the same roof. The different parts are connected and structured around a central zone which is developed over two floors. This central area houses the administration, production offices, dressing rooms and general employee functions.

The space sequence follows the industrial development of the auto which requires 1,900 workers to manage sophisticated computer systems and run mechanical equipment.

The floor that hosts management looks out on these same spaces from glass walls that permit managers to maintain continuous contact with the production phases and workers.

This layout facilitates synergy between different production sectors, collaboration between the various work teams and a comprehension of the entire system from an outsider's perspective.

The entrance is articulated by a triangular wedge that rises to roof level, a form that leads the eye towards the garden and at the same time controls the access flow for managers, workers and visitors.

The 700 square meter (7,500 square foot) hall opens onto the production area and functions as a social place for meetings, exchanges, and a place where tourists can orient themselves. This space, like the entire corridor, is illuminated from above with shed lighting-oriented towards the north in order to minimize heat introduction. The same design solution was chosen by Albert Kahn in 1909 for the first Ford factory constructed on a "T" plan in Highland Park, Michigan.

This zone is completed with a cafeteria capable of seating six hundred and fifty people which benefits from an enormous glass wall that opens onto nature: the water of the external pool, natural light from the sky and the Alabama woodlands enter and become a part of the edifice. The self-service café and the "wedge" at the entrance are accentuated through the reflection produced in the pool and by the paving resolved with small porcelain tiles. These same materials continue through all the flow spaces thereby characterizing the community areas.

External siding is resolved with rectangular white aluminum panels, a material that allowed for a reduced construction time, low cost and facility both of access and maintenance.

In addition to the factory there is a new Institute and Visitor Center constructed by Gresham, Smith and Partners which maintains a dialectic with the productive volume at a distance of 180 meters (595 feet).

This building is host to a variety of activities including client relationships, a tourist center, the Mercedes Benz museum and a training center for new employees.

Left, computer model.
The site was master
planned for future
growth, with the initial
facility occupying about
200-acres of the 966-
acre site, a former tree
farm. Below, site plan.

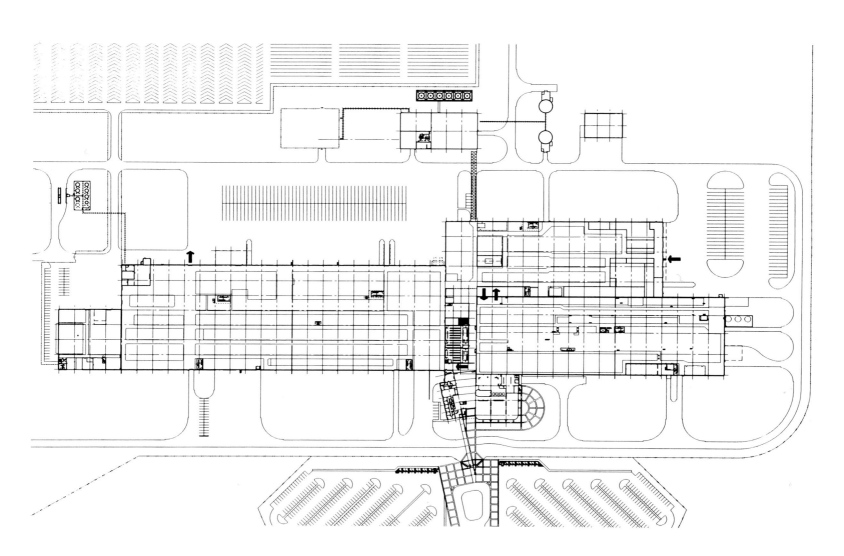

North-facing front
of the building uses
continuous, glazed
windows. The single
entry is marked by
a towering, triangular
metal entry feature
 or "prow".

Below, the visitor's lobby reception desk projects the classic, high-quality image of Mercedes-Benz, and is combined with warm wood paneling and supple leather case goods. Right, the atrium lobby is the focal point for the M-Class vehicle produced within the building.

Below, inspection and repair area of the paint shop. Opposite, finished vehicles enter the final inspection area.

Left, north-facing, sawtooth clerestory roof monitors rise eight feet above the roof line, allowing natural light to enter with minimal solar heat gain.
Administrative offices overlook the 41-foot-high atrium.

Opposite, the dramatic, 48-foot-tall entry "prow" serves to divert visitors to the left, through a separate set of doors to the visitor's lobby.

Ford Research and Engineering Center

A. Advanced Engineering Center (AEC)
Dearborn, Michigan

Completion date
1993

Owner
Ford Motor Company

Project Team
Ford Motor Company
Albert Kahn Associates, Inc.
Walbridge Aldinger

Photographer
Beth Singer

B. Dynamometer Lab Expansion:
Dearborn, Michigan

Completion date
December 1996

Owner
Ford Motor Company

Project Management Team
Ford Motor Company
Albert Kahn Associates, Inc.
Walbridge Aldinger
Interautomation Inc.
AVL North America, Inc.

Photographer
Christopher Lark

Located at the Ford Research and Engineering Center, the Advanced Engineering Center (AEC) presents a sophisticated container for specialized engineering systems dedicated to reducing noise and vibration in automobiles, guaranteeing comfort for the passenger and verifying engine and vehicle performance.

With these ideas in mind, a 26,000 square meter (280,000 square foot), four-story building was created, subdivided into 32 laboratories and 14 rooms for acoustic testing. The building was designed with an elevated level of flexibility in order to permit a rapid change in the internal layout. A wide range of tests can be carried out on everything from small car parts to medium-sized four-wheel drive trucks.

The laboratories house the preparative areas for the cars, with space for acoustic tests, vibration tests, and advanced laser holographic technologies. The work of 700 employees is structured on a model of continuous group activity with assiduous information exchange and interdisciplinary cooperation. This has simplified the hierarchical relationships diminishing problems among the personnel and conflicts inside the various specialized teams.

The building blends well with the traditional style architecture on the Research and Engineering Center campus, incorporating a brick-covered base with limestone accents and topped with metal wall siding and ribbon windows. This is exactly what Ford required in terms of simplicity of materials and architecture form. Completed in 1993 at a cost of 80 million dollars, the AEC has won six regional and national awards for design excellence and innovation.

An $8 million, 1,050 square meter (11,350 square feet) expansion to the AEC was completed in 1999. It contains a torsional vibration test laboratory, the first of its kind in North America. Test of vehicle engines and drivelines are conducted to evaluate noise and vibration characteristics. Sophisticated test systems simulate prototype engines for noise and vibration evaluation.

Additional growth at the Ford Research and Engineering Center is represented with the Dynamometer Laboratory Expansion, completed in 1996 for a cost of $120 million. The 14,500 square meter (156,000 square foot) lab is used for engine and powertrain development testing using state-of-the-art dynamometers and test equipment.

Albert Kahn Associates paid special attention to integrating the mechanical processes, electrical systems and building architecture with the test systems.

The lab contains thirty rooms in which tests can be run on engines and transmission systems. Half of these rooms are outfitted with climate control system where the internal temperature can be regulated to a minimum of -40 degrees C and a maximum of +110 degrees C.

With a total of 103 test cells in operation, the Ford Dynamometer Lab is one of the largest engine development and test facilities under one roof in all of North America.

Ford Dynamometer
Lab Expansion

Below, front entrance, site plan. Opposite, interior of powertrain environmental test chamber.

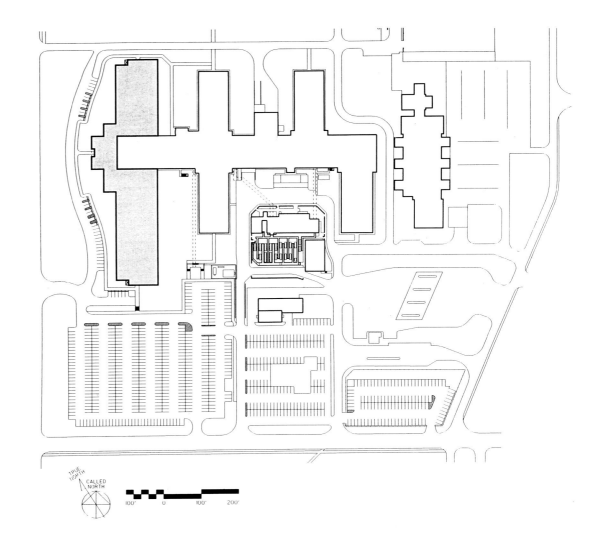

Ford Motor Company
Advanced Engineering Center

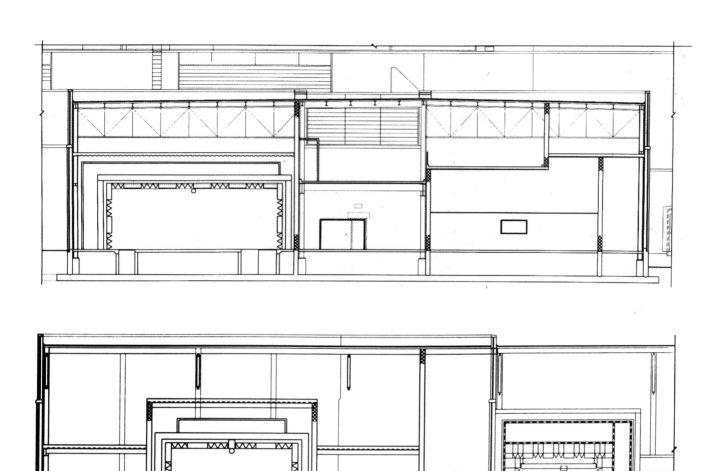

Opposite, sections.
Below, all-wheel-drive
chassis dynamometer
hemi-anechoic chamber.

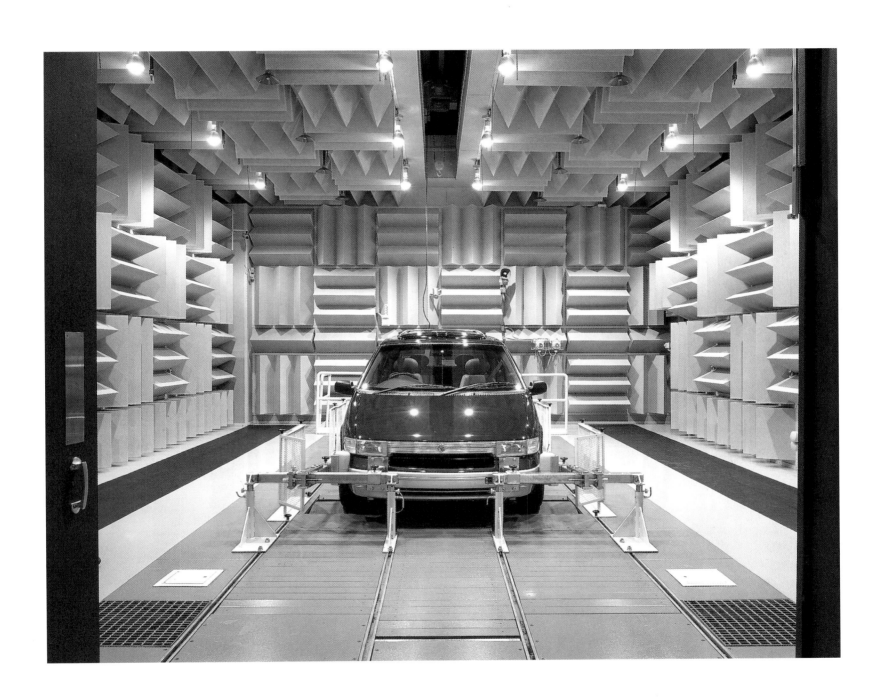

Left, four-wheel-drive, powertrain hemi-anechoic chamber. Below, engine hemi-anechoic chamber.

University of Michigan East Ann Arbor Health Center

Completion date
October 1996

Owner
University of Michigan Health System

Architect/Engineer
Albert Kahn Associates, Inc.

Landscape consultant
Johnson, Johnson, & Roy

General Contractor
Clark Construction Co.

Photographer
Gary Quesada @ Hedrich-Blessing,
Doriguzzi Photographic

The East Ann Arbor Health Center is located on the Michigan University east campus and offers a complete range of health services including general medicine, pediatrics, obstetrics and gynecology, internal adult medicine and family practice. There is also a diagnostic center, radiology, social services, a training center and a pharmacy.

The 7,000 square meter (75,000 square foot) institute was constructed on a 157 hectare (390 acre) property with the mission to treat patients while paying new attention to an atmosphere pleasant for both the patients and the staff. Other goals included supplying doctors with a functionary base in the community, supporting teaching in the medical school and programs in the research laboratories.

The objective of the project is consolidated in the hospital design which incorporated local forms and materials creating a link with the site, the community and the region. The project on the whole recognizes the natural beauty of the site, campus image and the importance of creating a family atmosphere. The design solution for the pavilions is structured on individual pavilions, with reduced measurements and heights, treated with the formal language of the regional tradition. The spaces between pavilions are resolved with flat-roofed arcades supported by brick columns with limestone details, enclosed by glass walls.

Development of the facade utilizes a base of limestone with particular attention to the bands of rough granite. A brick wall extends above the base for two stories, enriched by an alternating terracotta and limestone horizontal decoration which also forms the frame for the windows, reproducing the language of entire university campus. The hospital rests on a natural site and takes advantage of the slope of the land to create a complete southern exposure and minimize the height of the construction on its north face.

The complete design of the complex is based on a "T" form with an atrium at the center. This space is characterized by ample glass areas and manages the flow towards the various pavilions which are located on the wings of the T. Every pavilion houses a different specialization on each floor, each of which has patient admittance located next to the atrium. The internal layout is based on a two-corridor system with support functions in the center and patients towards the outside. Each medical room has a window which benefits from a view of the campus, helping to create a positive experience for the patient.

Services intended for the general public and visitors like the 24-hour emergency room, the pharmacy and the health education spaces destined for the community are located in the east wing on the ground floor in direct contact with the garden.

The layering of the building provides transitional exterior spaces including a formal plaza the opens to the site's natural features to the south. Split-faced granite provides an easily maintained surface at the ground plane.

Left, master site plan.
Below, floor plan;
patient care functions
comprise the wings
of the "T" plan.

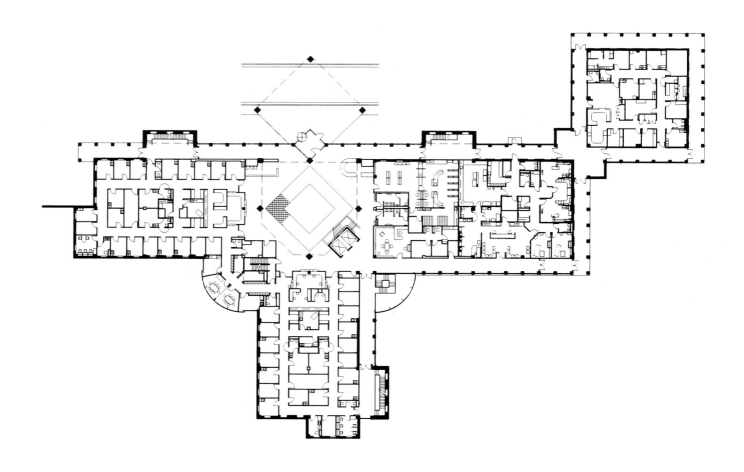

The atrium space is illuminated by ample glass areas, providing a wayfinding queu toward the clinic pavilions that are located on the wings of the "T".

Michigan State University Engineering Building Additions

Initial addition completed
1991
Second addition completed
1997
Architect/Engineer
Albert Kahn Associates, Inc.
General Contractor
The Christman Company
Photographers
Paul Bednarski, Glen Calvin Moon

The Engineering Building, built in 1962, has expanded to include two new volumes: one with an overall area of 12,000 square meters (131,000 square feet) and the second of 4,270 square meters (47,000 square feet). This expansion was completed in 1997 for a total cost of $14 million and houses the Grace A. Dow institute; a structure for composite material research, one of the first in the world dedicated specifically to these studies.

The total renovation has breathed life into the building volume with spaces for laboratories, classrooms, offices, and an engineering book center. Other specializations are included in the capabilities of the MSU research complex: road research functions; the station for experiments on self-propulsion and research on technologically advanced materials. The Engineering University, which in 1885 provided a single field of study, currently contains departments of agrarian techniques, chemical, civil and environmental engineering, information science, calculation engineering, electrical engineering, mechanical engineering and science. The university also houses a number of research centers and laboratories which promote interdisciplinary collaboration between respective faculty members, other universities and the public. The engineering library is situated on the first floor of the building. The resources include more than 80,000 volumes and over 500 current titles assisting research and the teaching needs of the university.

The three-floor building fulfills perfectly the client's two main requests: to integrate the ground floor of the old library, directly connected to the entrance, and to have acoustically isolated areas, both vertically and horizontally, in order to guarantee the liberty of the various activities undertaken in the space.

Materials used in the facade include brick and limestone which sustain a dialogue with the glass parts, which contain the vertical circulation zones and link the construction to preexisting buildings.

The second annex employs a different architectural language; externally it returns to the classic gothic collegiate style and internally develops extremely modern aspects, an alternation that creates a strong tension between the two spaces.

The facades are resolved with brown brick decorated with horizontal insertions of calcareous stone. This choice is also repeated in the south and north entrances at which, however, the position of the materials has been inverted.

The internal walls at the entrance are covered with stainless steel panels which create an exaggerated perspective. A similiar illusion is used on the ceiling which is resolved with a geometric pattern of copper panels alternated with a variation of brass panels. Brass insertions can also be found buried in the grey terrazzo flooring.

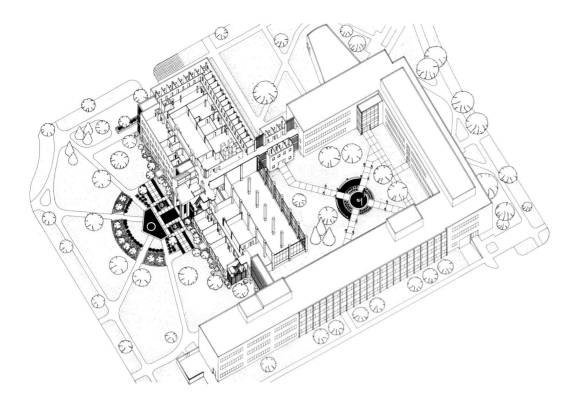

Left, axonometric.
Below, the courtyard
acts as the main
gathering space for
engineering students.
Opposite, south
entrance.

Left, south elevation. A combination of orange and red brick was used, with circulation areas identified by porcelain enamel panels and glass block. Below, site plan.

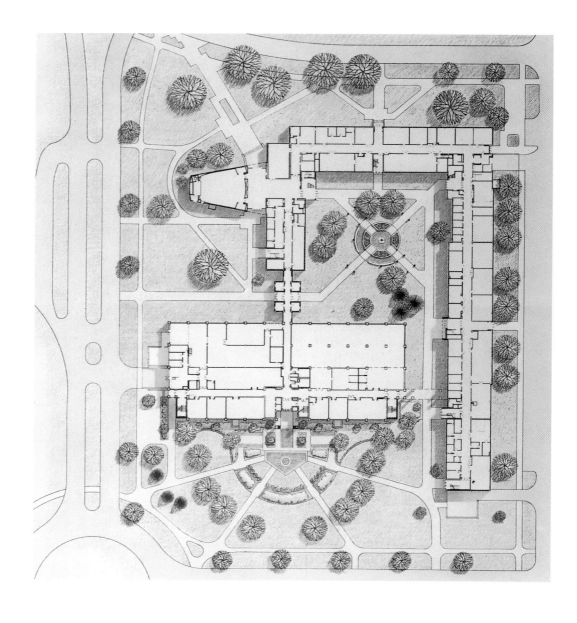

View across courtyard
to the two-story library.
The natural, mature
landscape is indicative
of the MSU landscape.

Left, the "link" building of the second addition. A ceiling geometry of aluminum panels of varying heights expresses the change of direction that takes place inside. Below, floor plans for the first addition.

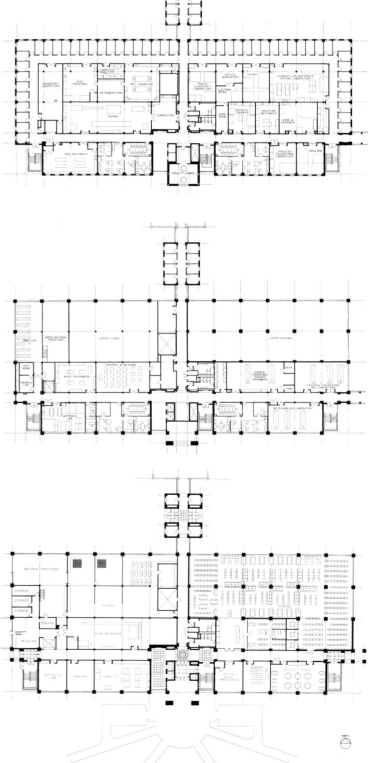

The circular window
of the teacher's lounge
provides the focal point
of the south elevation.

DaimlerChrysler
Indiana Transmission Plant

Completion date
August 1997

Architect/Engineer of Record
Albert Kahn Associates, Inc.

Interior Designer
Albert Kahn Associates, Inc.

Engineers
Albert Kahn Associates, Inc.

Landscape consultant
Albert Kahn Collaborative, Inc.

Food Service
E.F. Whitney, Inc.

A/V Consultant
Blue Water Visual

Industrial Waste Treatment
Traid Engineering, Inc.

Construction Manager
Walbridge Aldinger

Photographer
Christopher Lark

This large DaimlerChrysler factory is specialized in the construction of electronic transmissions for the new generation of Jeeps vehicles and Dodge trucks as well as for cars with posterior traction.

One billion dollars were invested in the construction of a 120,700 square meter (1.3 million square foot) plant erected on a property of 84 hectares (290 acres).

In addition to the factory the area hosts four other volumes: a 6,000 square meter(65,000 square feet) building for administrative offices for 125 people; a 3,475 square meter (38,000 square foot) edifice for service structures, a 1,210 square meter (13,180 square foot) building for treating waste materials and a 2,800 square meter (30,500 square foot) building for the energy center.

This new building was designed and constructed in just eighteen months. The initial planning began in August of 1995 and in November of 1996 production in the new factory was inaugurated. The first equipment was being installed while workers were still laying the pavement.

The complex underwent radical changes from the initial project: the added volumes were dealt with independently of the factory and expanded from their initial sizes; the 10 meter (34 foot) firewall was moved in order to make way for changes in the internal system. The glass windows were expanded in order to increase natural illumination and augment views of the surrounding panorama. In fact 80% of the productive volume has a seventy-centimeter (2 foot) window two and a quarter meters (7.25 feet) from the ground.

The factory was constructed with a modern respect for the site: the amount of underground tubing was reduced; the canals and waste tanks are enveloped in a double layer of protection. The vast woods completely encircle the volume intended for trucks hiding it from view from Highway 31 which passes nearby.

An in-depth study of the best work conditions was applied to the choice of materials and colors: white, clean offices improve employees' concentration and morale. The flooring is white and speckled with reflections, the areas with high personnel traffic and the entrance zones are colored a quartz blue.

When the factory reaches estimated maximum production it will employ 1,500 people.

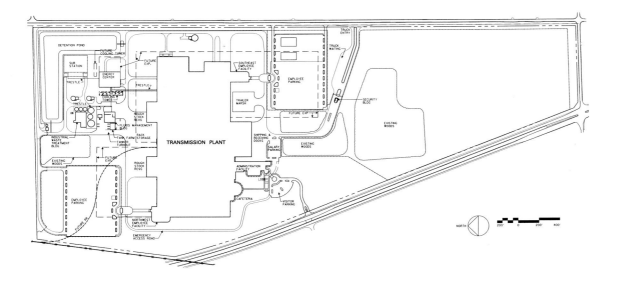

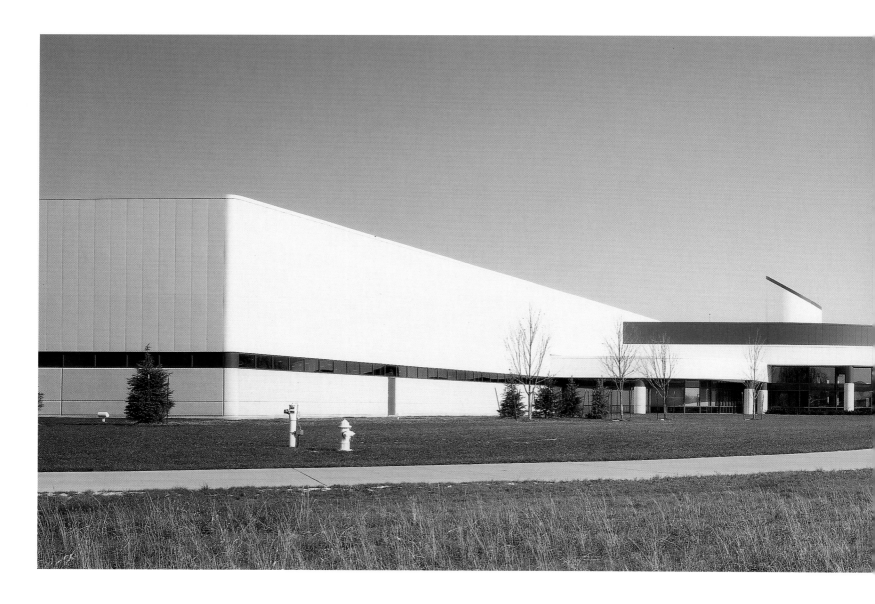

The 1.3-million-square-foot DaimlerChrysler Indiana Transmission Plant and administration building, looking east. Right, entrance to visitors' lobby. Left, site plan.

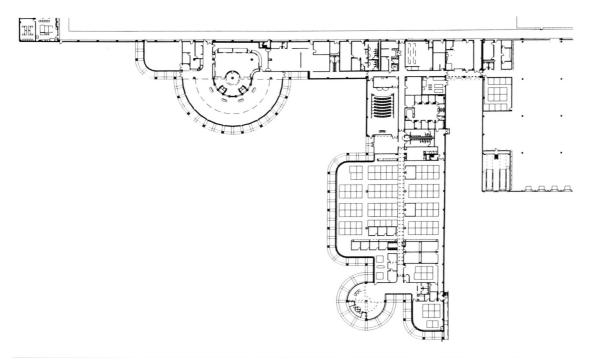

Below, the aisle that connects the visitors' lobby, office area and plant features a continuous, quarter-round skylight. Right, visitors' entrance lobby.

The cooling tower cells and main utility trestle serve the plant, energy center and other support buildings. Right, elevations, computer model.

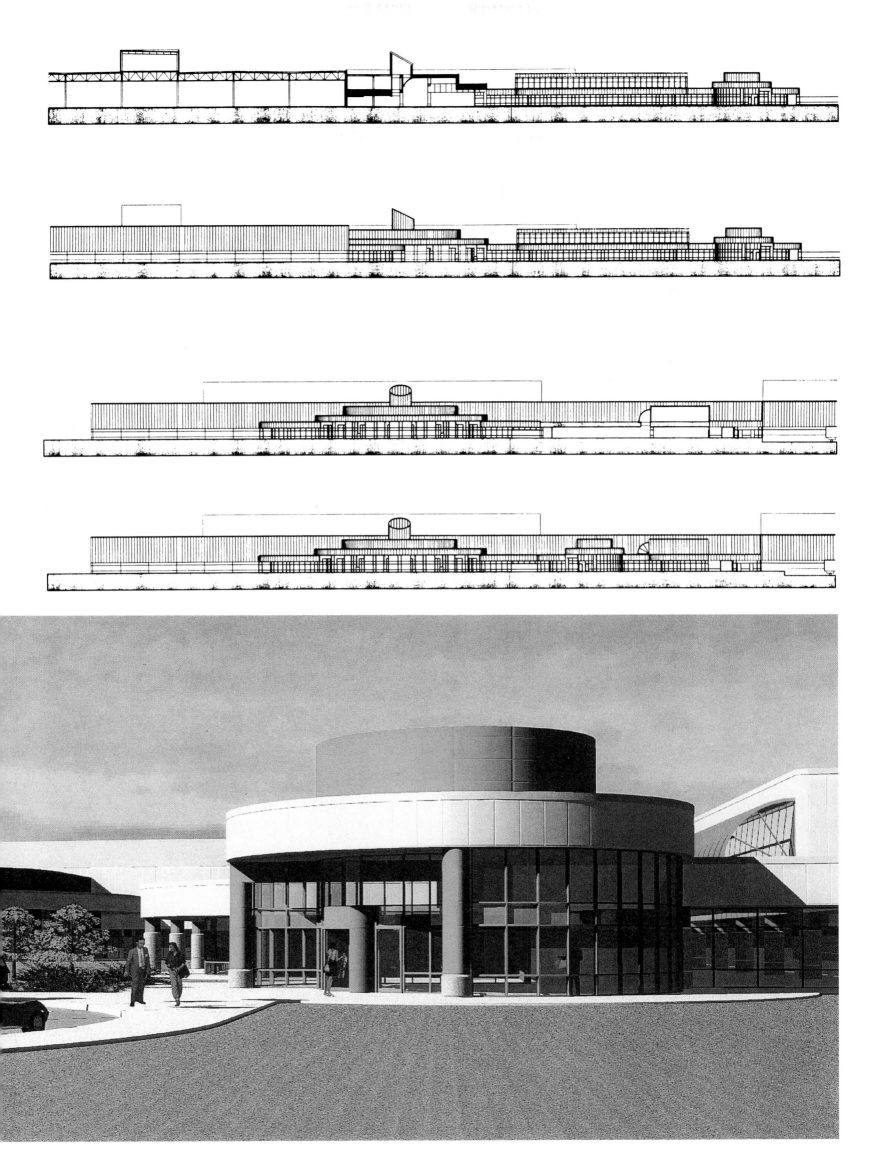

General Motors Building Prototype Wing 4A

Completion date
November 1997

Owner
General Motors Corp.

Architect/Engineer
Albert Kahn Associates, Inc.

General Contractor
LaSalle General Contractors

Photographers
Glen Calvin Moon, Christopher Lark

Considered by many to be the personal masterpiece of Albert Kahn, the General Motors Building initiated a new era in office building design. In 1919 GM founder William C. Durant commissioned the industry's leading architect Albert Kahn to create a new headquarters at the relatively unprecedented scale of 111,000 square meters (1.2 million square feet). Completed in 1922, the "Durant Building" anchored Kahn's New Center Area core, one of America's most successful urban ensembles. The subsequently renamed General Motors Building was added to the National Register of Historic Places in 1985.

In 1999, Albert Kahn Associates was retained to provide design leadership for the comprehensive renovation of the GM Building. The program accommodates State of Michigan regional offices in one of the largest adaptive reuse initiatives in the Midwest. Instrumental in the State's decision to revitalize the building was the prototype redesign for a single wing – "Wing 4A" – which demonstrated that the historic structure could be renovated to contemporary office design standards.

The GM Building's original plan includes four cross-wings extending from a linear service nucleus. Each finger-wing was designed for efficient layout, optimum daylighting and natural ventilation. The original glass and wood partition system brought both warmth and transparency to the typical office wing. Spacious eleven-foot ceilings with exposed ceiling/floor structure completed a rigorous modular geometry, articulated with spare detailing for its time.

The Wing 4A renovation prototype addressed a number of significant challenges that are generic to the historic adaptive reuse of office buildings. They included creating flexible office environments, projecting an image of progressive office design, integrating new building-wide systems and meeting current life safety standards, while respecting a landmark building's historic integrity.

The desire to restore the volumetric qualities of the original coffered ceilings was balanced against the need to modernize building services. The off-center column line anchors a multi-purpose service plenum that recalls the original closed corridor below and consolidates central air conditioning, electrical and telecommunication systems above.

Designed to evaluate a variety of workplace settings and proprietary furniture systems, the prototype interior addresses the growing emphasis on collaboration and teams. New alternative work environments were developed to support the user's evolving corporate culture and goals. Team centers, hoteling, free-address, and open workstations were designed for flexibility and future alternative reconfigurations.

Respect for the historical building has been the first objective, working internally without affecting the original look either of the internal walls or of the large windows. Wood flooring accents, stainless aluminum paneling, birch wood frames and details in openwork steel create a modern and sophisticated atmosphere that works well within the original Albert Kahn design.

Left, the original closed office environment exhibited both classical and early modern influences. Below, floor plan.

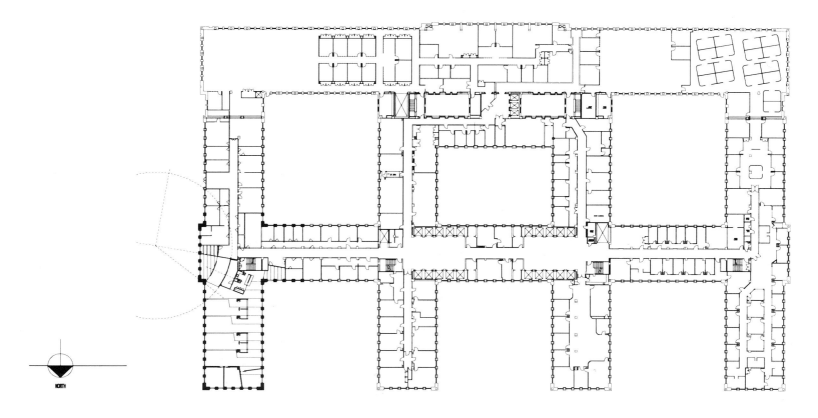

NORTH

Left, view from end of wing, with introduction of hoteling block. Below, teaming environment features windows revealed to their original head heights.

Left, perimeter circulation illustrates "cave" work environment, seen near window. Below, ceiling plan and floor plan.

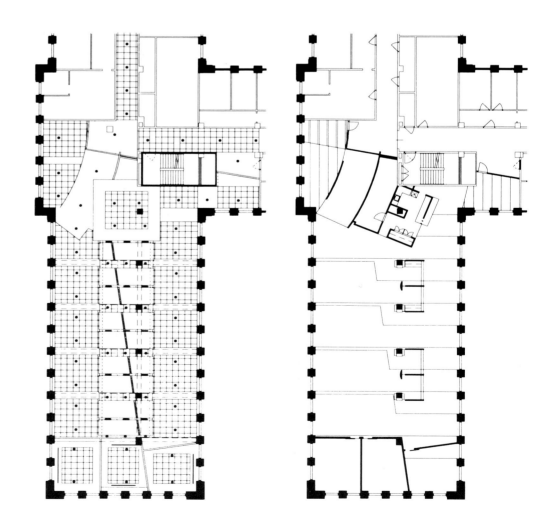

Grand Circus Park

A. Grand Circus Park

Completed
June 1998

Landscape Architect
Albert Kahn Associates, Inc.

Engineering
Albert Kahn Associates, Inc.

General Contractor
Posen Construction

Completed
September 1998

Photographer
Christopher Lark

B. Detroit Opera House

Completed
ongoing renovation/expansion

Architect - historical, interior
Albert Kahn Associates, Inc.
Architect -- stagehouse JPRA

Construction Manager
Walbridge Aldinger Co.

Mechanical & Electrical Engineers
SWS Engineering Inc.

Structural Engineer
Ehlert/Bryan Inc.

Plaster restoration
Commercial Interior Systems Inc.

Photographers
Christopher Lark, Laszlo Regos
Alan Lessing/Detroit News

C. Intermezzo Ristorante

Completed
March 1996

Architect
Schervish, Vogel, Merz, P.C.

Consulting Architect and Planner
Albert Kahn Associates, Inc.

Engineering
Albert Kahn Associates, Inc.

General Contractor
Turner Construction

Photographer
Christopher Lark

The Grand Circus Park, established in 1849, still plays a fundamental role in the life of the city considering its pivotal position between the Detroit business area and the Foxtown theater zone.

Collaboration between the projectual group Albert Kahn Collaborative and various city departments permitted the creation of a multidisciplinary project planned, financed and supported by different political components of the community.

The park extends over an area of almost 3 hectares (6 acres) and is in the midst of considerable development; renovations are taking place in the entire zone including the construction of two new stadiums–Tiger and Lions–as well as the recovery of the Opera House.

Two million dollars were set aside for the visual, esthetic and functional aspects of the project including all the primary categories necessary in an urban project. The two preexisting statues, one of Hazen S. Pingree and one of William C. Maybury have been uprooted from their original position and reinstalled north of the distributive axis of the park. Two six meter (19.8 foot) obelisks planned by John Piet and wrought from limestone have been placed in a central position, describing the southern entrance to the piazza and the alignment of one of the new accesses to the parking area.

The turn-of-the-century fountains–Edison and Alger–have been completely renovated, becoming esthetic focal points for the east and west sides of the park.

The work also provides for an amplification of flora, replanting the zone with trees, flowers, bushes and restructuring the irrigation system. For urban furnishing a series of eighteenth-century style lamps, modern cement benches and a carefully planned cement and paving stones have been added.

The new six meter (19.8 foot)-wide pedestrian road, finished with sidewalks partly dressed with granite, sustains a dialogue with the modern public transportation indications, the renewed road signs and the new bus area.

Two preexisting ramps to the underground parking have been removed and replaced with more modern versions. The same has been done with the old car exhaust removal systems which have been removed and renovated and made less evident from the outside.

Illumination for the fountains, the obelisks, the internal roads and the more suggestive zones have been emphasized in order to encourage Detroit's citizens to frequent the park by night. All the modern aspects have been intentionally mixed with eighteenth-century language to facilitate use of the park. The population has been given back their park, a modern and representative place that completes the urban reconstruction of Harmonie Park.

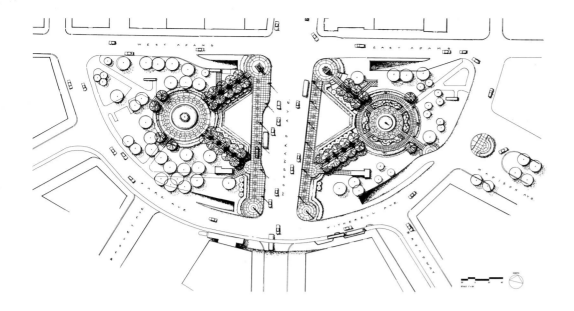

Previous page, the Alger fountain symbolizes the strength and integrity of Detroit. Reflecting the recreational, cultural, and historical significance of the city, the plaza lends itself to a myriad of public and private functions. Left, site plan. Below, the park highlights a symmetrical design of landscape and paving patterns.

Detroit Opera House

The Opera House was built in 1922 from a project by C. Howard Crane in pure European style with decorations that echoed the Italian Renaissance and ornamental details characteristic of Tiffany.

In 1985, after a devastating fire, the theater was abandoned to fend for itself and thus suffered further damage; left open to winter the water in the building's pipes froze and exploded causing extensive damage to the entire edifice.

In 1990 came the decision to renovate the entire central zone of Detroit and to restore the old theater, reproducing in their entirety the decorations from the Crane's original project. In spring of 1993, the destruction phase fell on the Grand Circus Theater in order to make way for construction of the new 7,000 square meter (75,000 square foot) performance stage.

The monumental reconstruction of the Michigan Opera House should be considered a key element in the economic, cultural and civic renovation of Detroit.

On April 21st, 1996 the twenty-fifth season opening and the inauguration of the theater took place with a gala concert including, among others, Luciano Pavarotti. The successive phases of the project include the construction and completion of a teaching center for artists as well as an area for administrative offices and two entirely glass-covered external elevators.

In June of 1996 David DiChiera, the director of the theater, announced the inclusion of great operas, ballets and special events over the course of the season representing all the artistic sectors with more than two hundred concerts.

The third and last stage of construction includes expansion of the foyer and the creation of a vast outside piazza for open-air concerts.

The theater has been decorated in Italian Renaissance style and completed with a multitude of turn-of-the-century ornamental elements: frescoes, brass details, colored windows in the ceiling, marble, mirrors and three sumptuous chandeliers reconstructed with 10,000 pieces of crystal. The damascus red typical of Italian theaters has been used for the curtains and principal draperies in accordance with the original project.

Even the 2,700 seats and the seventeen balconies have been faithfully reconstructed based on photos from the previous era just as the range of colors-blue, gold, red, ochre-are the same used in 1922.

Fourteen months of intensive labor employed numerous craftsmen in this faithful reconstruction of the grand theater, presenting the public with a refined and elegant edifice supported by high level of modernity hidden behind plaster and turn-of-the-century seating.

The annex which houses the backstage and the offices was resolved with an austere cubic volume with elements in reinforced concrete and supported by a steel structure that formally restates the rhythm, columns and characteristic elements of the eighteenth-century buildings that surround the Opera House and characterize Harmonie Park.

Far left, the auditorium and view of ceiling dome and proscenium arch from balcony. Near left, scaffolding allows plasterers and painters access to the arch; workers glue hand-painted canvas panels to the main arch.

Below, the theater's elaborate interior was restored to its 1922 gilded beauty. The cantilevered balcony contains a suspension arch that does not require support posts.

View of the main foyer connecting opposite street entry lobbies. The brass-and-cystal chandeliers are only three of 90 fixtures restored or reproduced. Below, left, detail view of restored vaulted arcade in the entrance lobby.Tiffany-style glass panels complement the rich palette of gilded ochre, browns and blues; right, the original carpet pattern was reproduced based on the fortuitous discovery of a small remnant. The imitation gold balustrade replicates the flamboyant original. Opposite, view of the grand tier boxes with doors that open toward main lobby. A subtle but magnificent feature is the restoration of the milk glass ceiling panels.

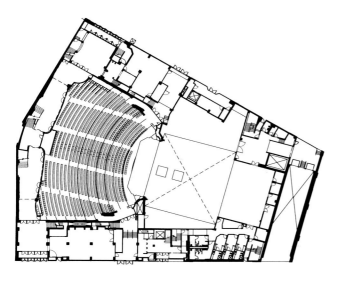

Left, floor plan. Below, the new stage house with rigging. The fly loft sores 85 feet high, the equivalent of eight stories.

Administrative offices. Selected as-found conditions were highlighted to provide historical context to the overall project.

Intermezzo

The Albert Kahn Urban Design and Plannig Collaborative is the projectual design and planning division of AKA, dedicated to territorial renovation of American cities. It is precisely this group of architects and engineers who undertook the vast project of renovation and revitalization of the historic center of Harmonie Park in Detroit. The park center–an old-world style zone filled with restaurants, art galleries, cafés and office spaces–has undergone important mutations in a few short years and is now aligned between the new entertainment areas of Detroit. Harmonie Park is characterized by a mix of decidedly modern elements and some of the best European-style architecture to be found anywhere in Detroit.

The project extends for almost 800 meters (2,640 feet) and includes the planning and construction of pedestrian areas, woody zones, public lighting and sidewalks; a new public center with restaurants, residential lofts, offices, shops, theaters, a directing studio and other buildings still under construction. The project reopens and highlights the zone surrounding the theater, taking advantage of the inherent drama of the site for the layout of lighting and the choice of colors.

The Randolph Centre, a building that dates back to 1898, is host to one of these renovation projects: Intermezzo. This 790 square meter (8,500 square foot) bar and Italian restaurant holds three hundred people. Ten million dollars were utilized for this construction and the renovation of five other turn-of-the-century buildings in which special attention was paid to restoring and maintaining the original materials: brick walls, maple flooring and wooden ceilings. The new sections were completed with modern materials.

The inside of the locale is characterized by industrial-style decoration: an ample open space interrupted by a series of columns; walls dressed with brick; a fifteen-meter (50 foot) wooden bar topped off with a rolling ladder to reach any one of dozens of bottles of liquor; a particular lighting plan and two murals created by the artist Jared Davis, a Detroit native.

The edifice also provides for parking on the ground floor along with the Italian restaurant and several warehouses for the shops.

This space is destined to maintain vitality and harmony between the theater zone and the park both at night and by day.

Located in the 1898 Randolph Centre Building is Intermezzo, an Italian restaurant and bar. Its vintage retail storefront put patrons on center stage.

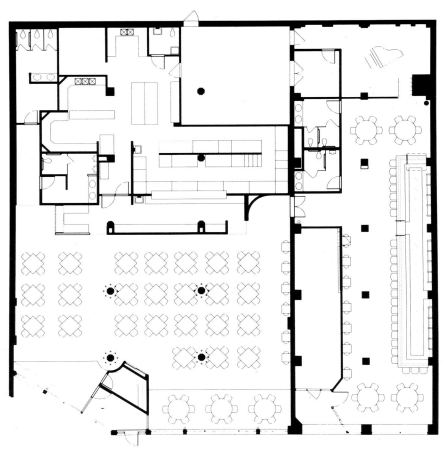

Left, floor plan. Below, the dramatic volume of the bar is exaggerated by the verticals of the liquor library. Opposite, monumental columns pierce the minimalistic form of the dining room.

Oakland University Elliott Hall of Business and Information Technology

Architect/Engineer
Albert Kahn Associates, Inc.

Construction Manager
Barton Malow

Targeted completion date
Fall 2000

The R. Hugh and Nancy Elliott Hall of Business and Information Technology located on the Oakland University campus is a modern edifice specialized in new information technologies. Through it, the university satisfies cultural requests of the new didactic programs.

Work on the complex required a $17.5 million investment and was completed in August 2000 based on a design concept with a high degree of modernity, flexibility and technology.

The 7,000 square meter (75,000 square foot), four-story school hosts didactic classrooms, a variety of information laboratories, six wireless rooms for internet connections, spaces for staff, administrative offices, meeting rooms for the students, television and audio production rooms and a 100 seat multimedia auditorium.

The materials used echo the formal language of the entire campus: open brick and stone with an abundance of windows allowing a high percentage of natural light to be captured. The north access, characterized by a glass "curtainwall", is presented in direct contact with the other university structures, connecting it to Varner Hall. To the west, the building is in close proximity to the Kresge Library. The entire southern zone opens through windows onto a forest panorama of the campus's wooded natural site.

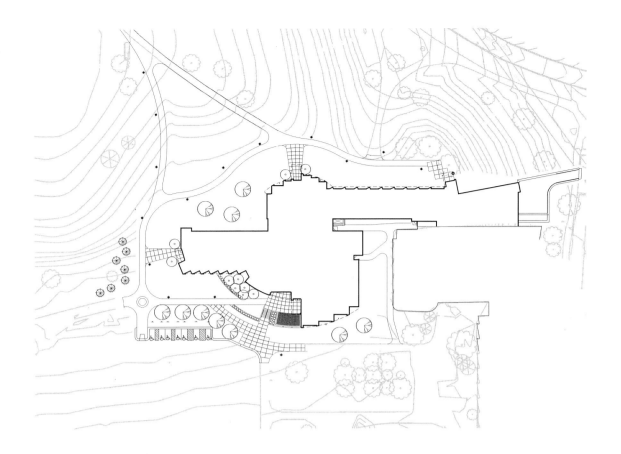

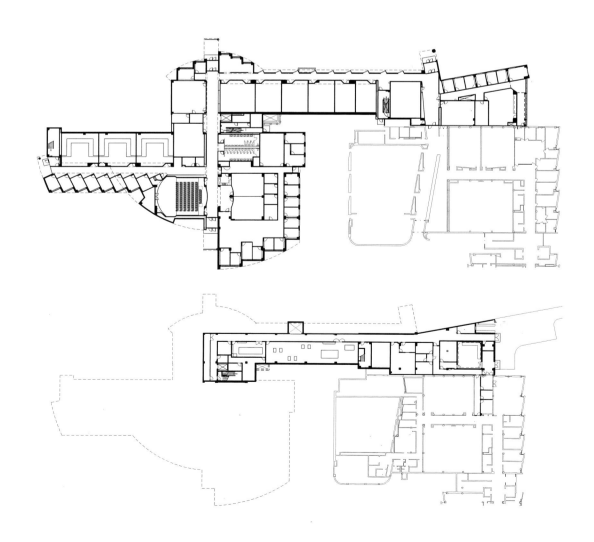

List of Clients

AC Spark Plug Company
AM General Corporation
A. B. Myr Industries, Inc.
A. J. Datlaff Company
A. Krolik and Company
A. M. Campau Realty Company
A. S. Norsk Maskinindustri
A. Simon & Company, Inc.
AIM Systems
APCOA, Inc.
Adler L. Brothers & Company
Ainsworth Manufacturing Corporation
Airlines National Terminal Service
Company, Inc.
Aladdin Heating and Cooling
Alden Sampson Motor Car Company
Alder L. Brothers & Company
Allied Signal
Almay, Inc.
Alpha Woodward Restorations, Inc.
Amalgamated Investment Company
American Axle & Manufacturing Inc.
American Blower Corporation
American Boy Building Company
American Can Company
American Electric Switch Corporation
American Electrical Heater Company
American Lady Corset Company
American Locomotive Company
American Motor Body Corporation
American Motors Corporation
American Radiator Company
The American - Scandinavian
Foundation
American Steel & Wire Company
American Steel Foundries
American Wire and Telephone
Company
The Amertorp Corporation
Amtorg Trading Corporation
Anderson Forge & Machine Company
Ann Arbor Savings Bank
Anne J. Kellogg School
Argonaut Manufacturing Company
Argonaut Realty Corporation
Arvey Corporation
Arvin Industries, Inc.
Assumption College
Atlantic Realty Company
Aurora Health Care
Auto Alliance International
Automotive Parts Manufacturing Co.
Autostroy Corporation
Aviation Manufacturing Corporation
Avon Products, Inc.
B. F. Goodrich Company
BMW Manufacturing Corp.
Bagley Building
Bamlet Building
Bank One
Bank of Detroit
Bank of Saginaw
Barbeque Grill, Inc.
The Barefoot Sole Company, Inc.
Barris, Sott, Denn & Driker

Barton Malow Company
Basch Company
Bates Manufacturing Company
Battle Creek Post Office
Bay City Library
Bay City Times
Bayer Brothers
Beck Engraving Company
Belle Isle Coliseum Company
Belmont Theatre
Bemb Robinson Garage
Berry Brothers
Bethlehem Steel Company
Betsy Barbour Dormitory
Bezner Alterations
Big Net
Birdsboro Foundry & Machine
Company
Black and Company
Blodgett Memorial Medical Center
Bloomfield Hills Country Club
Blue Cross / Blue Shield of Michigan
Board of Aviation Commissioners
Bodine Aluminum, Inc.
Bon Secours Cottage Hospital
Bond Clothing Company
Bond Stores, Incorporated
Book Cadillac Hotel
Booth Publishing Company
Borg-Warner Corporation
Boston University
Bower Roller Bearing Company
Boyer Stores & Garage
Boyer-Campbell Company
Boynton Stores
Briggs & Stratton Corporation
Briggs Commercial & Development
Companu
Briggs Manufacturing Corporation
Briggs Realty Company
Broadcast Design & Construction, Inc.
Bromley, F. L. Properties, Inc.
Brooker Electric Company, Inc.
Brooks Residence
Brotherhood of Maintenance
of Way Empl.
Brown & Brown
Brown-Lipe-Chapin Gear Company
Brush Estate, Union Trust
Bryant Apartment
The Budd Company
Buffalo Tank Corporation
Buhl Aircraft Company
Buhl Land Company
Buick Motor Company
Buick-Oldsmobile-Pontiac Division
Building Technology Associates, Inc.
Bureau of Yards and Docks, Navy Dept.
Burr Paterson
Burrell & Company, D.H.
Burroughs Adding Machine Company
Butzel, Keidan, Simon,
Myers & Graham
C. M. Hancock & Rivard Hall Lamp Co.
CB Richard Ellis

CBS CORPORATION
CSX Transportation
Cadillac Motor Car Company
Cadillac Plastic
Cadillac Square Garage Company
Caldell Wright Airport, Inc.
Campus Realty Company
Canadian Bank of Commerce
Canadian Bridge Company
Canadian Consolidated Rubber
Company
Canadian Hoskins Company, Ltd.
Capital Cities/ABC Communications Inc.
Carey Philip Roofing Company
Carford Company
Carharrt Hamilton
Caterpillar Inc.
Celotex Corporation
Central Savings Bank
Central United National Bank
Chalmers Country Home
Chalmers Motor Car Company
Charlevoix Hotel
Charter Township of Grand Blanc
Chas. B. Knox Company
Checker Cab Manufacturing
Corporation
Chesebrough-Pond's, Inc.
Chevrolet Motor Division
Chevrolet-Pontiac-Canada Group,
GMC
Chicago Mail Order Company
Chicago Motor Car Company
Chicago Pnuematic Tool Company
Children's Free Hospital
Children's Hospital of Michigan
Children's Orthopedic Hospital
Childrens Aid Society
Childrens Fund of Michigan
Chiyoda Automotive Engineering
Services
Chope-Stevens Paper Company
Christ Church
The Christman Company
Chrysler Canada, Ltd.
Chrysler Corporation
Cincinnati Milling Machine Company
Cincinnati Record Division
Citibank/IBM
Citizen's Insurance Company
Citizen's Title & Trust Company
City Auto Stamping Company
City of Denver
City of Detroit
City of Grand Blanc
City of Grosse Pointe
City of Hamtramck
City of Pleasant Ridge
City of River Rouge
City of Traverse City
The City Machine & Tool Company
Clark Equipment Company
Clarks Restaurant
Clayton Clothing Company
Cleveland Brewing Company

Cleveland Hippodrome
Clinton Memorial Hospital
Cloverdale Brewing Company
Cold Spring Granite Company
Colgate-Palmolive Company
College Club - Women's
Collins & Aikman
Colonial Laundry
Colt Industries, Inc.
Columbia Recording Corporation
Columbus Brewery Company
Comerica Bank Incorporated
Compass Management and Leasing, Inc.
Comprehensive Health Services, Inc.
Conelec, Incorporated
Congoleum-Nairn, Inc.
Consolidated Aircraft Corporation
Consolidated Cigar Company
Consolidated Tool Company
Consolidated Vultee Aircraft
Corporation
Consumers Power Company
Continental Aviation
& Engineering Corp.
Continental Motors Corporation
Cook Farm Houses
Cooperative Hospital Laundry
Corning Glass Works
Cottage Hospital
Couzens, Senator James
Cowham & Boardman
Crawford Door Company
Crittenton Hospital
Crocker-Wheeler Electric Mfg.
Company
Cronbie and Stanton
Crowley Milner Company
Crown Inn
Crudo Brothers
Cunningham Drug Store
Curtis Company
Curtiss-Wright Corporation
D & C Navigation Company
DMAX Ltd.
DSMA International
DURR/Rudolph-Libbe
DaimlerChrysler
Dalrymple-Morley Company
Dames&Moore
Daniel L. Bowers
Danly-Komatsu, L.P.
Darin & Armstrong
Davock & McCauley
Dayton-Wright
De Lorean Motor Company
Dearborn State Bank
Defense Plant Corporation
Defense Supply Service
Delco Remy Corporation
Delphi Automotive Systems
Delta Gamma House
Deluxe Motor Company
Denso Manufacturing Michigan, Inc.
Denso Sales Canada
Detroit & Ironton R.R.

Detroit & Security Trust Company
Detroit Athletic Club
Detroit Auto Specialty Company
Detroit Board of Education
Detroit Board of Public Works
Detroit Brass Works
Detroit Building Authority
Detroit City Gas Company
Detroit Creamery Company
Detroit Diesel Corporation
Detroit Downtown Development Authority
Detroit Economic Growth Corporation
Detroit Edison Company
Detroit Electric Company
Detroit Evening News
Detroit Forging Company
Detroit Free Press
Detroit Fuse & Manufacturing Company
Detroit Girl Scouts, Inc.
Detroit Golf Club
Detroit Harbor Terminals, Inc.
Detroit Home & Day School
Detroit House of Correction
Detroit Institute of Arts
Detroit Insulated Wire Company
Detroit Library Branch
Detroit Lubricator Company
Detroit Medical Center
Detroit Metropolitan Wayne County Airport
Detroit Mortgage Corporation
Detroit Motor Sales Company
The Detroit News
Detroit Opera House
Detroit Pressed Steel Company
Detroit Properties Company
Detroit Public Schools
Detroit Quality Brush Mfg. Co.
Detroit Racket Club
Detroit Renaissance, Inc.
Detroit Savings Bank
Detroit Seamless Steel Tube Company
Detroit Sheet Metal Works
Detroit Steel Products Company
Detroit Stoker Company
Detroit Times
Detroit Trust Company
Detroit Urban League
Detroit Wax Paper Company
Detroit Wire Spring Co.
Detroit, Toledo & Ironton Railway
DeVilbiss Manufacturing Company
Diamond T. Motor Car Company
Digital Electronic Automation, Inc.
Dodge Brothers, Inc.
Dollar Savings & Trust Company
Dolomite Materials Company
Dominion Sugar Company
Donnelly Corporation
Donovan Stores
Dow Chemical Company
Draper Motors Company
Durant Building Corporation

Durr Industries, Inc.
EE Linden Associates
Eagle Spinning Mill Company
Eastern Airlines, Inc.
Eaton Corporation
Eckhardt & Becker Brewing Company
Ecorse Foundry & Machine Co.
Edelweiss Cafe
The Edison Project
Edsel and Eleanor Ford House
Egyptian Government
Elgin Builders, Inc.
Eli Lilly and Company
Ellis-Don Construction
Empire Building
Engineering Power House
The Engineering Services Group
Espey, Huston and Associates, Inc.
Ethyl Corporation
Eurostar
Euclid Avenue Apartment
Evansville Bank
Everitt Motor Co.
Excelsior Supply Company
Fairchild Engine & Airplane Corp.
Fairview Savings Bank
Falls Springs & Wire Co.
The Farbman Group
Federal Aviation Agency
Federal Mogul Corporation
Federated Metals Corporation
Ferro Manufacturing Corporation
Ferry-Morse Seed Company
Fibre Package Company
Finsterwald Furniture Co.
Firestone Tire & Rubber Company
First Chicago - NBD
First Congregational Church
First National Bank
First National Bank of Lake Township
First State Bank
Fisher Body Corporation
Fisher Brothers
Flint Daily Journal
Flint Downtown Development Authority
Foley and Lardner
Ford Electronics and Refrigeration Corp.
Ford Exposition Building
Ford Manor Apartments
Ford Motor Company
Ford Motor Company of Canada, Ltd.
Ford, Henry
Fordson State Bank
Forge Shop Construction
Fort Dearborn Brewery Company
Fort Shelby Garage
Fort Shelby Hotel
Frank Brothers
Franklin Hills Country Club
Franklin Street Settlement
Frederick Stearns & Company
Freeman Delamater Company
Freudenberg-NOK

Freuhauf Trailer Company
Friesma Brothers Printing Co.
Froude Engineering, Inc.
The Fuller Brush Company
Fuller-Johnson Corporation
G & J Tire Company
GM Powertrain Group
GMAC
Gage Printing Company
Gannett Newspapers
Gar Wood Industries
Garden City Hospital Osteopathic
Gatley Clothing Store
General Dynamics
General Electric Company
General Motors Corporation
General Necessities Corporation
General Properties Company
Genessee Ramp Garage, Inc.
George Gorton Machine Company
Gerity-Adrian Mfg. Corporation
Ginsburg & Sons
Girls Friendly Society
The Glenn L. Martin Company
Goldberg Stores
Goodwill Industries of Greater Detroit
Gorham Tool Company
Gouddie Market Company
Grabowsky Power Wagon Company
Grace Hospital
Gramm-Logan Motor Car Company
Grand Rapids Evening News Building
Grand Trunk Office Building
Grant Memorial Tablet
Gray Motor Company
Great Lakes Engineering Company
Great Northern Cement Company
Greater Detroit Round Table
Gregory, Mayer & Thom
Grinnell Brothers
Griswold Building
Grosse Ile Airport
Grosse Pointe Country Club
The Grow Group, Inc.
Guardian Industries
H. Dreyfus & Son
H. Winston
H.P.F. Associates
Hackley Hospital
Haden Management/BOC - Willow Run
Haden Management/Dupont
Hague Apartment
Hall Improvement Company
Hammer, Siler, George Associates
The Hammes Company
Hammond-Standish Company
Hanes Hosiery Mills Company
Hannon Realty Company
Harold H. Clapp, Inc.
Harper Hospital
Hart Manufacturing Company
Havenwyck Hospital
Hayes Manufacturing Company

The Hayman Company
Hazel Park High School
The Heald Machine Company
Health Alliance Plan
Heinz, H. J. Corporation
Henry & Wright Manufacturing Company
Henry Ford Health System
Henry Ford Hospital
Henry Ford II Residence
Herchede Hall Clock Co.
Herman Keifer Hospital
Herman Miller Inc.
The Hertz Corporation
Hevenrich Building
Higgins Industries
Highland Park General Hospital
Highland Park State Bank
Himelhoch Bros.
Hines Interests Limited Partnership
Hinkley Motor Corp.
Hiram Walker & Sons
Hirschman, J. F. and I Stores
Holcomb Robertson
Holley Carburetor Company
Hormel & Co., Geo. A.
Hotel Addison Company
Hotel Pontchartrain
The Houston Chronicle Publishing Co.
Houston Housing Authority
Howard Young Medical Center
Hudson Motor Car Company
Hudsons, J. L. Company
Hugo Scherer Estate
Hull Building
Humber Limited
Hupp Motor Car Company
Hurley Medical Center
Huron Portland Cement Company
Hyatt Roller Bearing Company
Imperial Distillers Products
Independence Cigar Factory
Industrial Engineering Services Inc.
Industrial Works
Ingalls Health Systems
Intasio Building
Interautomation, Inc.
International Harvester Company
International Steel Company
Investment Properties Corporation
Iron Ox Company
Isuzu Motors, Ltd.
JBG/TrizecHahn
Jackson City Hospital
Jacobs Manufacturing Company
Jennison Hardware Company
Jewish Community Center
Jewish Home For The Aged
Jewish Institute Auditorium
Jewish Old Folks Home
Jewish Womens Club
John Deere
John Ladd Manufacturing Company
John Lauer Machine Shop

Rouge Steel
Rudolph/Libbe Inc.
Rushmere Club
S. S. Kresge Company
S.E.A.T.
SG Construction Services
Saginaw Club
Salvation Army
Samuel Francis Smith
San Telmo Cigar Company
Saulsenette Lych
Scherer Estate
Schloss School
Schoenborn & Cowles Manufacturing Co.
Scholastic, Inc.
Schuler Incorporated
Schust Company
Scott & Jones
Security Trust Company
Seiberling Rubber Company
Senator Alger
Senior Investment Company
Sesco Incorporated
Shaarey Zedek Temple
Shaw-Walker Company
Sheller - Globe Corporation
The Sherwin-Williams Company
Siegel Paint Shop
Sigma Nu House
Sikorsky Aircraft
Silent Automatic Corporation
Simon & Company
Sinai Hospital of Detroit
Sloane-Blabon Corporation
Sloman Building
Smallwood Brothers
Smith, C. F. Company
Smith, Joseph N. Company
Sorensen
Sorisis Chapter House
Southeastern Junior High School
Southfield Downtown Development Authority
Sparrow Health System
Spartanburg Steel Products, Inc.
Spaulding Manufacturing Company
Spicer Group
Spiegel Zamecnik & Shah Inc.
Spietz & Worch
Spitzley Corporation
Springfield Body Company
Springman Paper Products Company
Square D Company
Srere Brothers
St. Francis Home For Orphan Boys
St. John Health System
St. Joseph Hospital
St. Mary Hospital
St. Mary's Church
St. Paul's Parish
St. Vincent Medical Center
Standard Accident Insurance Company
Standard Auto Company

Standard Club
Standard Fruit Company
Standard Motor Truck Company
The Standard Products Co.
Standard Tube Company
Stark-Hickey Co.
State of Michigan
Stearns Stores
Steel Products Company
Still Memorial Osteopathic Hospital
Stinson Aircraft Division
Stormfeltz Loveley Company
Stott Realty Company
Strauss Land Corporation
Stroh Casting Company
Studebaker Corporation
Summerfield & Hecht
Suomi College
Superior Match Company
Surgicon Inc.
Sverdrup Technologies
Sydenham Glass Company
TAC Manufacturing Inc.
Taber Cadillac Company
Talon Development Group, Inc.
Taylorcraft Aviation Corporation
Teledyne Continental Motors
Temple Beth El
Temple K.K.B.Y.
Texas Fair Cafe
The Thomas Henry Simpson Memorial Institute
Thompson Aircraft Products, Inc.
Thompson Auto Company
Thompson Center
Tillow Garage
Tixon Corporation
Todd Shipyards Corporation
Tokai Rika U.S.A., Inc.
Toledo Scale Company
Toledo Shipbuilding Company
Tonawanda Coke Corporation
Tower Automotive
Tower Realty Management Corporation
Toyota Motor Manufacturing, NA, Inc.
Toyota Technical Services
Tractorostroy
The Trane Company
Trans Pacific Stores
Travis Pointe Country Club
Triangle Publications, Incorporated
Trinity Medical Center
TrizecHahn Office Properties, Inc.
Trumbull Memorial Hospital
Truscon Steel Company
Trussed Concrete Steel Company
Tuller Hotel
U. S. Aviation Field
U. S. Department of The Air Force
U. S. Department of The Army
U. S. Department of The Navy
U. S. Government
U. S. Motor Test Sheds

U. S. Savings Bank
U. S. Signal Corps.
U. S. Aviation
UAW-DaimlerChrysler
UAW-General Motors
Union Drawn Steel Company
Union Trust Company
United Aircraft Corporation
United Air Lines
United Aircraft Corporation
United Hebrew Charities
United Jewish Charities
United Savings Bank
United States Coast Guard
United States Parcel Post Bldg.
United States Savings Bank
United Technologies, Inc.
United Wallpaper Factories, Inc.
University Apartment
University of Detroit Mercy
The University of Michigan
University of Michigan Health System
University of Nebraska
University of Notre Dame
University of Toledo
Upjohn Company
Valeo
Van Husen
Vendome Hotel Building
Veterans Administration Hospital
Vincent Garage
Vinton Building
Visteon Automotive Systems
Volkswagen do Brasil
Volkswagen of America, Inc.
Von Weise Gear Company
Voplex Corporation
W. H. Edgar & Son
W. H. Mullins Company
W.F. Hall Printing Company
WJBK-TV Detroit
WTVS/Channel 56
Wabeek Corporation
Wadsworth Mfg. Company
Walbridge Aldinger
Walker Block
Walker Stores
Walker-Saxe Motor Company
Walkerville Ferry Dock
Walkerville Golf Club
Walkerville House
Walkerville Post Office & Town Hall
Wallace Laboratories
Warren Hospital Corporation
The Washington Post Company
Washtenaw Community College
Watson-Zumstein Company
Wayne County
Wayne County & Home Savings Bank
Wayne County Community College
Wayne County Medical Association
Wayne Hotel
Wayne Public Warehouse, Inc.

Wayne State University
Webster Cigar Company
Weil Company
Welded Steel Barrel Corporation
Welt Stores & Apartments
Westinghouse Electric & Manufacturing Co
Wheeling Church
Whirlpool Corporation
White Motor Corporation
White Star Navigation
Whitehead & Kales
Whitney Realty Co., Ltd.
Wick Building
Willard Storage Battery Co.
William Beaumont Hospital
Wills-Lee
Winkelman & Harris
Woodlawn Cematery
Woodward Mid Cities
Woodward Realty Co.
Worman Motors Ind.
Wright-Patterson AFB
Wright Aeronautical Corporation
Wurtzberger Store
Wyandotte Hospital and Medical Center
Y.W.C.A.
Yondotaga Club
Youngstown Hospital Association
ZF Batavia, LLC
Zuchelli, Hunter & Associates, Inc.